Soul Mate Love

Soul Mate Love

Inside secrets

from an
Authentic Soul Mate Couple

Shannon & Scott Peck

Soul Mate Love
Inside Secrets
from an Authentic Soul Mate Couple

Copyright © 2018 by Shannon & Scott Peck

Lifepath Publishing

1127 Santa Luisa, Solana Beach, CA 92075

Cover by Killer Covers

ISBN-13: 978-1984265975

ISBN-10: 1984265970

Dedication

This book is dedicated to
every person yearning for
soul mate love

Table of Contents

Chapter 1

New Soul Mate Love Openings on Earth

As we become more aware of the influx of greater light into our hearts and consciousness, we are also becoming acutely aware that the potential openings for love are also greatly increasing. It feels like a new time is approaching.

Our completion of "Soul Mate Love: Inside Secrets from an Authentic Soul Mate Couple," has been a surprise to us. We weren't planning to write another love book. And yet, a few months ago, it was as though we were tapped on the shoulder by a divine impetus with the idea of this book.

The interesting thing is that, for 25 years, we have written about love and relationships. But we've never been able to put into words the phenomena of our personal love. It has surpassed any description – until now.

We know there are so many people looking for a soul mate and the quality of love that comes with it. Hearts have been aching for a long time on earth, each one knowing that only a higher type of love can fulfill the ache.

Spiritual people are having a hard time staying grounded without deeper love. We are getting the feeling that now, as there are so many grand awakenings within the collective consciousness, it is logical that there would also arrive a grand awakening about love.

We find it odd that few authors have written books on the subject and so little is known about soul mate love, the kind that we two share and want for you. It's not widely taught.

And when it is, it's generally by a single author and you don't see the model of what this phenomenal love looks like and how it acts differently.

And yet, there's a powerful energy field around soul mate couples who practice being on their soulful purpose together through soul mate love. There's an expansion quality of exponential love which occurs. That's why we've always called it phenomenal. Almost indescribable – until now.

We have had the feeling for quite a while, that when we hear people say they yearn for soul mate love, and they can't describe it (like us, until now), that they aren't sure what it is.

Let us give you a metaphor. If we pointed to a gigantic warehouse full of toys, cooking appliances, roses, and a million other things. And we said, "There's a carburetor in there. Can you please locate it and bring it outside the warehouse, so we can discuss it?"

We feel that most people would wander around in the warehouse without a clue as to what it is they are actually looking for. They heard the name. They have an idea of its size. But what exactly does it look like. How could you possibly find it when you haven't actually seen one?

That's the way it is with soul mate love. You need a picture, a detailed description. You need to understand its dimensions and weight and color, etc. Now you have an idea of what it is you are looking for. And the chances of finding it have just increased dramatically, right?

Well, we've cracked the code on the description and depth and dimension of this most special love on earth. And we have discovered that we can bring to you the phenomenal love bubble in a way that you will get it.

Throughout the book, we have described it, listed what the qualities are, offered personal stories, and even ended with a chapter called "Quantum Soul Leaps," just in case you want even more! And some of Scotty's drawings and poems are added as further dimensions to take you there.

We have been guided to write this book as though the words flowed from a source that is love itself. Sometimes the best things in our lives occur when they weren't even planned. The information in this book came as a revelation. The inspiration poured out.

And for you, this will mean a real look into what soul mate love is and, we hope, will describe what you think you have been yearning for all this time.

And for couples who already have an extraordinary love, we think you'll be given insights to dial it up to the next levels. It's good news for us all!

And, one more thing. In our vision of what is occurring on earth with the light and energy surges coming rapidly into consciousness and our hearts, we feel that the love that will soon be pouring in is going to take everyone to a new level. It will become easier to find this love and to have it as your personal experience!

In our 25 years of sitting in the love bubble of soul mate love, we have experienced a presence and companionship of love itself.

We have also found that it greatly softens the human experience and even brings healing. It's a new way of managing the human experience, with soul mate love. You'll see! And we can't wait for you to have it!

Get ready for the spiritual experience of your life!

Let's call in this love together!

The Secret to Falling in Love
by Scottyg

Let's see...
What have you learned about love so far?
Well, it often hurts
And it is often absent
And it is ridiculously hard to find or keep

Yet my heart so yearns to be loved
And I present myself, I think, quite nicely
Is there a secret I don't know?
I sure would love to be in love

This is so important that we should consult
an expert
Let's ask Love
Love, what is the secret to finding love?

No secret at all my sweetheart
I've been your lover since the moment you
first thought of love
Ecstasy is so much closer than you imagine

So far, however, you seem only
to have flirted with me
No matter at all
I'll never stop waiting for you
to fall madly in love
with Me

Chapter 2

Soul Pain

Living without love is painful to the soul.
We both know.

If you are yearning for soul mate love – for the real thing – we hope our stories will give you hope and confidence and, more importantly, greater love wisdom - the wisdom neither of us had before we met.

Scotty's story of soul pain

For the first half of my life, I was not at all love savvy. I was a loving person, but had no idea, really, what soul mate love even was. I just expected love to work.

That's how I entered my first marriage. It seemed like right attraction. We worked together and had the same passion for education. And we had fun together. It seemed right.

Over the next few years, however, the relationship deteriorated. I felt pressured to be someone I wasn't. As the marriage evolved, I felt more and more abused emotionally. I felt I was deeply stuck in a marriage that I could never exit. Fear kept me bound. This misery continued for seven years.

This was not the love I expected or hoped for or thought would naturally occur. The ending was abrupt. I finally developed the courage to leave.

One would think that this unhappy love experience would have shaken me wide awake to a higher love consciousness, but it didn't. I was relieved to be free of the painful experience, but I soon found myself in another relationship. And yes, I got married – for another miserable seven years.

How could that possibly happen? Even her father said to me, "I can see why she wants to marry you, but I can't see why you would want to marry her." Yes, her father said that to me! And I, of course, in my continuing lack of love wisdom, absolutely ignored his words.

This marriage was miserable in a different way. My wife was indifferent to me and very self-centered. My need for love & affection was completely unmet. How could I be back again in a painful intimate relationship? Love ignorance, that's why. Just imagine feeling unloved and ignored in your marriage for seven years. That about sums it up.

One day, I said to her, "Our marriage is not working - for either us. Are you willing to work on it?"

Her immediate answer was "No."

My heart actually felt relief with that answer. It was a final curtain call to the misery. I wondered why in the world I had waited so long to ask this vital question. Her answer gave me the impetus and courage to take the initiative for divorce. It was amicable – because I made it so.

So, there I was, alone now in my house and deeply relieved. My soul was out of prison. I thought to myself, "I never want to be married again. I would rather be single for the rest of my life than ever gain live in love pain."

As the next year unfolded, I found my heart slowly evolving to a different place. I found myself thinking, "Geez, I'm a deeply loving person. It doesn't make sense for me not to have success in love."

I was waking up to a higher understanding of love. I thought to myself, "I deserve to be with someone who loves me just as much as I love her." It's embarrassing to admit, but this is the first time in my entire life that I had even thought of that obvious love standard. I found my heart expanding as I discovered - within my soul - that I deserved such love.

I wasn't in a hurry to meet anyone. In fact, I wasn't even dating. But my love consciousness was shifting to a higher place. Alone, but happy, I just kept listening.

And then, one day, my view of love shifted exponentially. I thought to myself, "Yes, I deserve to be well loved, but this is even more than a desire. It's really my spiritual right to be loved this way." Wow! Was I actually thinking this?

Yes, I was. My love awareness was reaching upwards towards soul where my inner substance as a spiritual being was being seen and honored. I thought, "If this is true, I don't need to do anything but just let Soul unfold what's next."

At this time, something very synchronistic occurred. I lived in San Diego, but I was invited to help develop a workshop in Los Angeles for teenagers called "Living Love." We were expecting about 1,000 participants.

I drove up to Los Angeles every week for several months to help plan the event. Our goal was to address needs such as suicide, abuse, loneliness, drugs, & dating by having the teenagers experience the power of listening, non-judgment, and unconditional love. I was invited to train the facilitators who would lead these small-group sessions.

I thought to myself how crazy it was that everyone seemed to perceive me as a love expert even though I had been a failure at love in two marriages. I knew within my own soul, however, that I was deeply engaged with love itself. I am passionate about love.

And that passion was rising to a higher place. During one of the training sessions I was conducting for the facilitators, a woman in the back of the room stood up and asked me a question. I have no idea what the question was, but I immediately felt myself feeling, "I'm going to marry that woman!" I've facilitated a lot of workshops and never had such feelings.

After the session, I asked someone who that woman was. I was told that she was married. I thought, "My intuition sure is way off."

Well, it turned out that she was actually divorced, but this person didn't know it. Several months later, I called her, asked if she remembered me, and asked if she had time to talk. She didn't. She was on her way out. "Could you call me at another time?" "Sure," I said.

Truthfully, I had no intention of calling again. It felt like my intuition was off. But you know what? I wasn't grasping for love. I knew now that I deserved to be deeply loved. In fact, I thought to myself, "I'm a deeply spiritual man. I deserve to be in a relationship where my soul mate is as spiritual, or MORE spiritual, than me."

My understanding of soul mate love was finally taking shape within my own heart and consciousness – after more than 40 years of love blindness.

Months later, Shannon and I finally met in person. From the moment we met, we were both ecstatic. But Shannon not so much as me! We had a blast dating, but Shannon was still reeling from her failed marriage. Could she trust my love? These were underlying fears but the developing joy in knowing each other was stronger.

I remember a significant turning point in my own soul mate love awareness. I told Shannon, "I want you to have all the love you deserve, but if your love for me is not as real as my love for you, it's better we both let go. I don't want to be in a relationship where I am loved less than I give love myself."

Inside my heart, as I shared those words, I felt like I was giving away the most treasured opportunity of a lifetime because I was deeply in love with Shannon. What the hell was I doing?

What I was doing was taking a stand for soul mate love for myself. My willingness to let go of Shannon, for her happiness and also for my higher well-being sent waves of awareness to Shannon's heart. It brought us closer, not further apart.

Unlike my previous marriages, this one began on the foundation of soul mate love. I can't wait for you to learn more.

Shannon's story of soul pain

Skipping ahead, I can tell you that Scott and I raised our own vibrational levels so high that we called each other into our soul mate fields. Here's how it happened.

When my husband left me, after 18 years of marriage, I went through a period of grief and devastation. He not only moved out, but I discovered a deep secret he'd been hiding from me. He was in love with another woman.

All he could think of was to get rid of me. How did all this come about? And who was this woman that I was losing my husband to?

After he left, and in ensuing weeks, for the first time in my life, a deep hatred grew within me. I was consumed by the thought of them being in love, living together, working together, laughing, and having intimate moments. He had even made her president of our company, the company I had helped to grow & support as it grew into a global business.

I had never experienced such jealousy and hate in all my life. How could I live with it! I was miserable. I could hardly think of anything else. It had to be cleared if I was to go on with my life. I'm normally a happy person who lives in harmony. This was a crazy me I had never seen or felt. It was overwhelming, and I had to find a way through it.

There was a turning point through much prayer and contemplation when I saw no other way than to love them. I prayed to love them both. That was a big moment and a turning point. It didn't come right away.

But soon after this prayer, I was given an image of them as babies in a mother's arms. In this image, I was their mother. I could see their innate innocence and purity as little babes. And I could love them as though I were their mother. I saw this fundamental goodness as their true selves. I found that forgiveness would come in no other way.

Little did I know, at the time, that this was my spiritual preparation for meeting my beloved soul mate, Scotty. When we met, I came with far less baggage, having cleared my anger.

After this clearing, I began contemplating a desire for marriage. But how on earth would I ever find someone, the right one, to marry? Was there a someone for me? I certainly didn't want to date.

I had been giving serious, deep thought towards how I wanted to correct my poor choice of a husband for the future, should I come into the situation of being in love again. I needed to know where it had gone wrong and what I could do to make it right.

I listened for divine guidance which I'd always trusted. Those divine answers sometime come in odd ways!

One day, as I was thumbing through a magazine, I came across a full-page picture of two cows, one licking the other one in nurturing love. I stared at the picture for a long time, then thought to myself, "I'm always the licker. I'd like to be the one who's being licked for a change! That's what I need!"

I've always been a big giver. And I was realizing, for the first time in my life, that I also needed to receive. I had needs too! The picture became a treasure and a symbol for the direction I needed to take. It represented what I had learned during a mostly unhappy marriage.

I tore out the picture and taped it on my bedroom bookshelf so that, every time I saw it, I'd be reminded of what I most needed in an intimate relationship. I had to learn to protect myself and to change this old habit of being the licker! This goal became active in my consciousness.

Here's the picture I looked at every day for many months, until Scotty, a huge giver, came along.

Chapter 3

What is
Soul Mate Love?

If you did a random survey asking a million people if they wanted to meet their soul mate, our guess is that the answer would be a resounding "Yes!"

Yet most people have not experienced soul mate love - or even been around it. And, although there are zillions of ways of expressing love within a relationship, it is our intention to be completely transparent with you about our own soul mate love as well as how it's changed over the years to the present high point of identifying and living with each other as souls.

So let's have a discussion about what soul mate love is – and isn't - so we can open some of the doors and windows and let it start shining its light on you!

Here's the first soul mate secret:

**You can't take "soul"
out of "soul mate"**

Without soul, a relationship may be happy, or even deeply loving, but it won't be soul mate love.

In soul mate love, it's more than two humans connecting in love, as wonderful as that may be. It's two conscious humans who are discovering their souls connected in passionate interest and caring for each other with an uncanny desire to be together all the time. As they come together, they find themselves on an unending soul journey.

Soul mate love has the extraordinary power of influencing who you are as an evolving soul. It's life transforming. It brings forth your Higher Self like nothing else. Trust us. That's what you want.

There are very few opportunities that bring forth your Higher Self in a relationship. But soul mate love tends to lift us higher than just the human realm, to a place more extraordinary with love than you can imagine. That's what we experience.

Looking back, we can't even begin to believe that we have now been together for the last 25 years. It feels like we just got started! The love has deepened us to unimagined heights of bliss and fulfillment. And it has brought to light our souls, or Higher Selves, which were far fainter before we met. This is the power of soul mate love!

Guess Who Love Is

by Scottyg

*I've been waiting for you to ask me about
love
But I can no longer contain
my soul
My soul is blazing Love's Radiance
Do you feel it?
You will
It is permeating into you like invisible
magic
Quietly
Inescapably
Deliciously
Completely
So now the most delightful question
Can you guess who Love is?
I can
Love is announcing Herself
As You!*

See your love life as part of your soul path

Everyone is on a soul path, whether they know it yet or not.

Your soul came here because it has vitally important things it wants to learn and express. In the process, it experiences what it's like to be a human who forgets you are a soul, who is clouded by an ego that makes you believe that you are only a tiny dot in the universe, a person who is struggling and often suffering, trying to have a better life.

As an exercise, try making a list of turning points in your life and the top things you learned and ways they most changed you. This gives you the perspective of a soul who came here to learn and grow. It also reveals if you learned from the turning points because, if you didn't, it will most likely be repeated. And, again, you will suffer until you get it. This eventually acts as our motivation.

Our previous marriages are good examples. Scott didn't learn the lesson after his first marriage & he endured more love pain. But he sure did learn the soul lesson after the second marriage!

Often our life goals are about getting an education and a good job, marriage, being loved, having children, gaining financial security, wonderful friends, and a lovely place to live. Yet, your soul is on a very different mission.

Your soul has a life purpose to fulfill – something you probably feel deep within, even if it's partially hidden.

It is with this consciousness that you enter a soul mate relationship. This is a sacred relationship where you can rise to greater heights of spirituality.

It's a place where, through great humility towards Spirit, you turn to this divine source many times a day to make sense of everything and to gain guidance, which you hold as vital, sacred, and holy.

It's where you practice immense gratitude and recognition of the guidance received with a devotion to follow it to the ends of the earth.

The reason that soul love is different than other love relationships is that you are taking on the perception that both you and the person you are loving is a soul who incarnated with the purpose to grow in Spirit. When two people who are in love do this together, it takes on a dimension that is beyond this world.

In the process, you are discovering more of your soul essence and their soul essence, what lies behind each of your life motives, and the depth of caring and love within your bond of unity.

If each of you is dedicated to the soul path, you are growing as your relationship develops, since the human experience tends to be bombarded with challenges. A soul rises to meet such challenges in spiritual ways. This is soul mate love.

It may begin with a strong attraction towards something very special you see about each other and then, over time, develop into soul mate love.

How to recognize if you're in a soul mate relationship

You know you are in a soul mate relationship if:

- You easily, and passionately, love each other.
- You are eager to be together endlessly.
- You naturally fit with each other.
- You have a strong interest in each other.
- You recognize that each of you love the other with a love that's bigger than both of you.
- You want to offer support towards each other.
- You have an uncanny number of things in common.
- You have an incredible feeling of deep, loving connection.
- You can't imagine loving another person more! Nor can you imagine being more loved!

- You are on a spiritual path – you read spiritual books, have "meaning of life" discussions, pray, reflect, practice mindfulness, and share from your depths.
- You are deeply committed to each other.
- You feel there's so much more to come through sharing your life with this person!
- You open your heart to deeper sharing than you've ever known, and you feel safe doing so.
- You experience love that is dependable, reliable, and consistent.
- You experience your love mate caring for <u>you</u> as much as for himself or herself.

When we first began discussing this book, we identified what we each felt are some of the main qualities for soul mate love. Here's what we wrote in the first 2 minutes:

- Loving kindness.
- Connection to each other's soul or Higher Self.
- Deep respect for each other.
- Openness to soul, to the bigger and greater part of you, which is mostly hidden.
- Honesty and truthfulness.

- Giving and helping.
- Patience.
- Heart-centeredness.
- Listening, understanding, & empathy.
- Humor and play.
- Equality,

See? This isn't hard stuff!

We don't want to keep this definition of a soul mate relationship on a narrow level. There are many ways lovers connect. In fact, in many relationships, one person may be a talker while the other is not. What happens then?

In such a case, the relationship will rely on the unspoken connection. It doesn't always take words to bring you together. Our energies can delight in unity regardless of words spoken.

Sometimes, by taking delight in your soul mate, the way he or she treats others, the way he or she loves you and has special qualities that you are in awe of, both hearts feel this extraordinary appreciation and love. It has a way of filling the space. It feeds the relationship.

Some couples connect deeply through touch or time together on walks and in nature, or through strong mutual interests. These are ways that nurture the relationship as well. Notice how you best connect at deep levels. Frequency is the key here. Your connection needs to be felt ongoing.

Just as our bodies appreciate a couple good meals a day, so do our hearts.

So, when you aren't a talker, be aware that you will need to show up daily with great love, attention, and acknowledgment. It could turn into a problem if you love your soul mate but fail to find ongoing creative ways of showing it. This is what keeps love alive! This is what we all live for!

Love needs to be nurtured and encouraged. If neglected, just like a plant without water, it shrivels and dies.

How do you know if it's not soul mate love?

Here are the clues:

- The opposite of lovingkindness is apathy, anger, or insensitivity.
- The opposite of connection to each other's soul, or Higher Self, is intolerance, judgment, and a disgust or lack of interest in soul or Higher Self.
- The opposite of deep respect for each other is arrogance, disrespect, bullying, and control.
- The opposite of openness to soul, to the bigger and greater part of you, which is mostly hidden, is a heart closed to evolving higher.

- The opposite of giving and helping is taking & being uncaring.
- The opposite of patience is annoyance, exasperation, harshness, and pushiness.
- The opposite of heart-centered is coldness, indifference, and discord.
- The opposite of listening, understanding, and empathy is being ignored, failing to have your heart heard, or even your words. It's a lack of caring about you and your soul.
- The opposite of humor and play is seriousness, tension, or rebuff of your joy.
- The opposite of equality is someone who thinks they deserve more than you – more talking time, more decision making, more control.

It's impossible to live life without encountering toxic behaviors. Some relationships are so filled with this that the relationship itself feels toxic. That's probably because it is.

Sometimes our hardest relationships are within family. Use these relationships to deepen and refine your love skills and your ability to forgive, including yourself.

Sometimes we are so lost in love that we can't see the big picture. Because we want it so badly, we tell ourselves that we're in a soul mate relation-ship. Don't try to make a toxic relationship into a soul mate relationship.

Soul mate love is not toxic. In fact, it's the opposite. The opposite of toxic is loving kindness, honoring, and respect. Stay awake and be honest about the quality of all your relationships.

To create space for soul mate love, evaluate your top 5 relationships

It's not easy to assess a relationship when you're in the thick of it, but remember, you are on a soul path. You are awakening to your Higher Self. You deserve a mate who can share this path with you.

So, take an honest look at your five closest relationships:

- Which of them would you place in a category of great love shared by each of you?
- Is one of them among your best ever friends?
- Which of them do you most cherish and why?
- Which ones do you tolerate?
- In which ones are you the giver and they the taker?

- How much value or pleasure does each relationship actually give you beyond occupying space in your life?
- Which one do you regard as a friend, and yet they don't really fulfill the requirement of being a true friend?
- To what extent are you connected in soul or a spiritual quest?
- Which one, do you feel, knows your soul?

Perhaps, after this evaluation, it's time to make room for some new friends. And if there are those on your list who you realize are truly a wonderful friend, it's time to acknowledge it so that they know how much – and why – you value them.

Can you have a soul mate relationship if you or your love mate are not on a spiritual path?

- When spirituality isn't acknowledged, soul mate love usually isn't present, except in hidden ways. This doesn't encourage self-realization and all the wonderful things that come from soul mate love.
- Soul mate love is kind. Kindness is spirituality in action.
- Mindfulness practices are profoundly spiritual and can connect you to a

realm of awareness that is essential to soul mate love.

- Sensitivity to others' feelings and tuning into their hearts can create good will and intimacy which are ingredients of soul mate relationships. This is the spiritual path.

Of the wonderful conversations we'll be describing, where we've reached pinnacles and felt supported to go forth and rise even higher, these things occurred because we were flowing with open, ongoing spiritual values, personal acknowledgment, mutual desires, and valuable insights from our practice of awareness.

The purpose of a soul mate relationship is to so identify and love each other's soul that this encourages you to become more visible, (even to yourself), where you can come forward and express yourself deeply. You rise in self-realization and love.

What is so healing about these relationships is that, because of the immense motivation to love even more, the ego has less strength. As you rise in your Higher Self, the ego diminishes more and more.

So, the answer comes back to our first secret. You can't take "soul" out of soul mate. If you do, you may have a happy, even wonderful relationship, but it won't be soul mate love.

There are many forms of love

Love comes in many, many forms. There are thousands of happy couples who love and adore each other and have harmony. These couples are elevating the world.

Many relationships are fulfilled in the joy of raising a family together. Many just enjoy each other's company & shared life moments. Many have mutual interests, like sports, music, art, nature, or hobbies. Many couples enjoy traveling together.

All these forms of love can be fulfilling and full of genuine love, even though there might be little interest in exploring soul. That's okay. Soul mate love is not everyone's desire. We respect that. In fact, our life motto is: "Many paths. One love."

If you're in a relationship that is not yet drawn to soul, you may find an evolving desire to take your love life even higher. Or you may find yourself as the partner wishing your mate would open more to soul. If so, you'll find many ways, in this book, to increase the value and quality of your shared love.

How Intimate Would You Like to Be with Love?

by Scottyg

*How intimate would you like to be with
love?
This is really
the only question worth asking
Would you like your soul to be caressed by
love?
Would you like to be
Known, admired, cherished?
Would you like to be lifted above all
doubt, shame, & fear
Replaced entirely by knowing how I see
you?
Would you like to
play & laugh & relax with me?
Would you like to look into my eyes
& exchange only love?
How intimate really
would you like to be with love?
"Entirely," you say
but how can I possibly experience such
love?
The answer might surprise you
You just did!*

Chapter 4

Loving
Your Soul Self

When was the last time you acknowledged your soul? Or another's soul?

Maybe reading this book is opening you to a new place, where, for the first time, you are acknowledging that your soul exists. But what does that mean?

Acknowledging your soul promises and delivers great hope for love. It has a way of expanding your life. It inspires you to new heights, living as a soul, thinking out as a soul, connecting to yourself as a soul.

It opens you to a new way of viewing yourself and others. It enlarges your spirituality and consciousness. It's a big deal.

Let's look at two choices of how you can look at yourself and for leading your life.

You can go through your life primarily in ego consciousness where you think of yourself as a mortal who is trudging along by yourself - alone, anxious, wanting, worried, hoping, striving, sometimes happy although mostly stressed, or needing to be right and to pronounce yourself and your opinions, feeling pressured, needing to feel important and loved and belonging, comparing yourself to others, feeling insufficient about money, the future, and just about everything scary you can think of.

Or, you can go through your life at a far higher level where you are acknowledging yourself as a soul. In this more elevated state of consciousness, you discover an entirely different way of viewing yourself, as a divine self who is empowered because you are from a divine origin.

From this elevated place, you move into your heart and feel whole. You naturally love yourself.

The burden of the ego gets lifted the more you view your soul self and love it. Even connecting with your soul once a day or periodically through some days gives a lot of silence to the ego and a great rise to your true soul self.

Another name for your soul is your Higher Self. Here are even more ways to describe your soul:

- Sacred self.
- Divine self.
- Divine nature.
- True Self.

Are you drinking this in?

Your Higher Self is your soul. It's not just the part of you that lives forever. It is the reality of your whole self and is the ticket to ultimate freedom to all the love you could ever want, forever. Please don't deny yourself this love!

Living as a human means you have taken on the illusion that you are a material being, living in a body, which dies. This is the context of your entire human experience. It looks as though everything comes to an end, including your life and identity.

Yet, the discovery of Higher Self, or soul, places you in an entirely new context where the real you is no longer the one in a human body who is subject to the ultimate fate of mortality.

Since your soul is the realization of Spirit as the only true reality, you join that context, and everything in your human life is now colored by that context of you, temporarily in a body, but governed by your eternal soul, which consciously lives forever.

It's the ultimate state of self-realization. By knowing your soul, you naturally love yourself.

In fact, it's a love state of mind which is part of your vast forever. There's no ego present to object and make you feel guilty or ashamed for loving yourself as soul. The soul becomes quick to drop the ego, as the ego is the false sense of self.

Your soul self is, perhaps, the onset of the most powerful awakening you can encounter in the human realm. It's your human connection to the divine You. You discover that there is an inner voice which, when you listen to it, is your guide. It enables you to live outside of the normal scope of limitations, where we self-limit for a million reasons.

Your Higher Self opens you to the potential of all love and all healing possibilities. It fulfills your human life to its greatest possible extent. It's your light! And it carries a powerful attraction field!

By placing your Higher Self in charge of your life's direction and guidance, you open your intuition to empower yourself with answers that you could not otherwise access for going forward successfully.

Your Higher Self is the source of all wisdom and it unlocks deepest truth.

Your soul is your Higher Self which begins to answer the imperative questions:

- Who am I?
- What is my purpose?
- Am I living my purpose?
- How can I be successful and become all that I am meant to be?
- How can I find my soul mate?

Who Are You?

by Scottyg

When you look beneath your atoms
what do you see?

When you ask your heart
"Who are you?"
what does she say?

When you open your mind
what are you actually opening?

"Who are you?"
is actually a rather tricky question

I can save you an eternity of wondering
Like the essence of a flower
Let your Soul
do all the talking

Grow into your soul and find even more love

Think about your spiritual growth and evolution. The version of yourself ten years ago is no longer who you are. That person is gone.

Your present version of you, as wonderful as it may be, is just as temporary, because you're evolving all the time. In the age we presently live in, there is almost unprecedented massive amounts of stress and rapid change that we must cope with, creating great conflicts with pressure to move through them.

This is the perfect scenario to grow and it requires the learning of skills which, when practiced regularly, will help to lead towards greater enlightenment as well as inner peace and balance, an area where your soul picks up a beautiful glow.

Here are some of the ancient skills (many of them Buddhist) we have learned and put into daily practice and which help to offset the daily and ongoing challenges of living in these times:

- Letting go.
- Non-clinging, non-attachment to outcomes.
- Breathing in peace.
- Staying in the present moment.
- Mindfulness.
- Equilibrium.
- Forgiveness.

- Observation of thoughts & emotions & desires.

We practice awareness, trying to be alert to evaluate our thoughts during a conflict, asking, "Is this thought from the ego? Or from the Higher Self?"

We make strong efforts to practice non-identification with the ego's ongoing drama, releasing it, and remembering to simply be. These are strong practices!

Plus, we try to practice unconditional love which is devoted and passionate towards seeing the innocence of each other's souls, ourselves included, and which quickly discards blame, guilt, and shame as intruders to this goal.

In addition, we love to pray, which consists of asking and listening for guidance and connecting with Spirit. This sacred relationship with the divine is key to our lives, our souls, and our love. It is how we evolve in soul mate love.

How do you view yourself? Mostly as a human with a soul? Or mostly as a soul who is having a human experience?

The difference in these views is vast, like comparing night to day. It's your soul that carries your light, love, power, joy, and capability. Why were we never taught this? And if it is true, that you are primarily a soul, living a human life, how can you come to realize this more fully?

Here are a few ways you can discover your soul or Higher Self:

- Be open to the real you as a soul. Welcome and accept it.
- Ask Spirit to help you.
- By-pass the ego's judgment and criticism. Your soul or Higher Self is pure, innocent, and beautiful, without exception. Your Higher Self is full of goodness!
- Make a list of your best qualities, which represent your divine goodness. (e.g. loving, caring, compassionate, patient, kind, peacemaking, giving, fair, tender, merciful, calm, open, etc.) Allow your list to come quietly, intuitively. Ask Spirit to help you. Which qualities do you most relate to? It doesn't mean you are always this way, but it means that this characterizes you and you recognize yourself in these qualities.
- This list represents what you carry in your heart, even when you mess up. As you dwell on how important these qualities are, they will grow and evolve.
- Have a conversation with your Higher Self and ask it to become known to you. Let Higher Self answer.
- As you identify others' Higher Selves, you get better at recognizing it for yourself. Recognizing it, you are honoring it.

Most people don't recognize it. The more that Higher Self is recognized, the more it becomes confirmed and validated for you. It's an invitation to become more pronounced and visible.

- What are your biggest gifts? What have you most given to others? What have others said about your positive effect on them? What effect do you suppose this is having on the planet? The universe? The collective consciousness?

The more you address and drop anger, resentment, hurt feelings, fear, and identifying with your human story, while asking for your soul to become known to you, the more your soul will become apparent.

This is the big work. It also enables you to love yourself in beautiful ways. What a relief it is when we stop criticizing ourselves and start noticing our wonderfulness! We are free to love ourselves!

When you change the context of seeing yourself, less as a human and more as a divine being, the Higher Self surfaces and becomes more visible to you.

The soul lives very close to Spirit, it's source. It does this by asking for guidance. When there's trouble, we go to Spirit, and ask, "What am I being guided to see or to do? How is my soul being guided to view myself or this situation?" When you ask Spirit, there's always an answer. Be sure and listen to the answer.

Going to divine Source, the Creator and Origin of all life and love, you can't go wrong asking for divine guidance in every situation. The only you that exists is the divine one. This is what it means to love yourself!

You'll find yourself vacillating from viewing yourself as a soul and viewing yourself as a human. With the entry of our human experience came amnesia about who we truly are. But we can, with practice, learn to recapture our true, divine self.

This is the soul's path, to remember who we truly are. And once you start remembering, there's no end to your discovery. It's amazing! Persistence wins the prize of living as a soul on earth. This also creates enormous appreciation and love for your true – and only - self.

When you view yourself as a soul, it leaves out the ego, the self that believes it's all alone and is desperate for love. It's a relief to turn to your soul, which is on a spiritual path and wants to connect with its divine roots, again and again.

To surrender the ego to the divine Self is the path of enlightenment. The ego insists on being right. It believes it isn't good enough and that it has to compensate for this by pretending it is better than it is. It lacks confidence and believes it must compete for anything good. It believes it's unlovable. It lives in a dream world full of negative emotions, always struggling, seeking to feel better, wanting. It causes the soul to recede and become unnoticed.

The ego forgets that the human self and human experience are a dream. It's a lonely life as an ego. Each time you remember yourself as a soul and begin to tune in for divine guidance, it connects you to your Source as a soul. Things begin to rapidly change for the better.

This is what it means to live consciously as a soul. And this is where you are most likely to find a soul mate. Usually, we don't pick them. They just show up.

Let soul, not ego, inspire and guide your love life. And, if you're not yet in a soul mate love relationship, get good at soul dating.

Chapter 5

Soul Dating

If it were up to us, everyone would be with their soul mate and experience this extraordinary love. The world would be incredibly better off if we were all called into the field of soul mate love. Perhaps, this is where we are heading.

Before we met, Shannon's husband had left her for another woman. As she grappled with her new life, she addressed the fact that she still would prefer to be in a marriage even though her marriage hadn't worked out well.

She attributes the following prayer to finding Scotty. And it happened shortly after.

"Dear God, I want to be in a loving marriage and with the right person. I want it with all my heart. But, you know me. I don't have a clue as to how to go about finding this person. I'm not good at these things. I don't want to miss out on this opportunity. I'm asking you to bring him to me from the ends of the earth, wherever he is. Bring us together. I will remember that this is being fulfilled whenever I think of how much I long to be in a loving marriage."

After this prayer, she felt her part had been done. And, whenever fear entered, she remembered her prayer of trust and power and reminded herself that she was praying to divine Love, the very source of all love. As far as she was concerned, it was the finest thing she could do. Either it would happen, or something even better would occur.

Scotty feels he was also divinely prepared to meet Shannon. We both attribute divine guidance to finding each other. Soul mates finding each other is a divine event.

This is how the distance of our lives was bridged. To us, it was nothing less than a miracle. Based on the high standard each of us was not willing to lower, we each wanted a mate that would love us as much as we loved them. Is this so hard to do? We had come to a point in our lives where it was going to be at this level or nothing at all.

We had each reached for a higher source to solve our problems for us. And we were blessed beyond our wildest imagination. This higher frequency, calling in the love you deserve, has a way of attracting at a higher level. It's powerful, because your soul is involved.

After speaking at conferences, we have heard from people who told us, that once they had seen our soul mate model, they were able to attract their soul mate to them. It got easier once they saw the model. We hope that this book will be your model and that you will also find it easy to attract your soul mate.

After all, as souls, we are created for love! And a lot of it! Even though you may have been raised in unloving circumstances with apathetic or angry parents, or siblings who were cruel, or you felt completely invisible or unimportant, (we've all had some of that, right?), it may influence you humanly to feel discouraged about the prospects of love in your life, but, we assure you, it doesn't influence your soul and its naturalness to love and be loved. And your age doesn't matter!

Begin with a prayer. Your soul knows how to call in your soul mate. You already made this arrangement before you arrived on earth. Remember? And you two arranged for a synchronistic moment when you would meet. There are no accidents.

We two didn't have our synchronistic meeting until we turned 46 years old after divorces. Humanly speaking, we would have both loved to have met far earlier, before the hard marriages. But our souls had another plan.

We aren't suggesting that your soul has planned misery for you prior to your awakened love together. Looking back, Shannon can see that the years of difficulty in her marriage accounted for an immensely important time for her soul to step up into her warrior mode as a healer. She had to in order to remain sane in the marriage.

She seized the moments during those years which also were teaching her, "If this is what makes me miserable, what would make me happy?" It was a steep learning curve, especially as she had to continually release anger and resentment. She grew a lot and she learned tons!

Scotty trudged through two previous marriages before we met. His soul was also on a mission, one of learning to love himself and to learn to be absolutely true to himself, to take action towards moving in a direction that he most needed towards a loving relationship.

There's lots happening during years that look like a wasted failure. It isn't a waste, as long as you learn lessons, which is why you are here. And these lessons of great wisdom and insight are what act as a powerful draw to attract your soul mate. Soul mates find each other through their soulful growth patterns, and it makes them beautiful in every way.

What if the one you are dating won't commit &, God forbid, isn't the one?

If the one you are dating isn't the one, there's nothing you can do that will make it happen.

Acting out of fear or being desperate to be loved, won't change anything except creating awkwardness and a faster breakup. This is a moment for your soul to be noble. It isn't personal. Either it's a match or it isn't. And when it isn't, you need to know that as well.

While dating, and before you know if this is the one, keep your focus on enjoying this person and learning about their soul. Honor who they are. See how love and appreciation develop the relationship in a beautiful, harmonious way.

It may be just friendship in the beginning. We think there's no finer start to a soul mate relationship.

If it becomes a best friend relationship, that's a strong step towards a lasting relationship. Give it time. And as you do, treat each other's hearts with great respect. This is a soul you are dating. It isn't a grab-me relationship where you need this person to fix everything in your life by loving you. That isn't the behavior of your soul. Get in touch with your beautiful, balanced soul and act in accordance.

Hope is important. You wouldn't want to live your life without it. Yes, go ahead and hope that this is the one. But hope with the understanding that it may not be the one and you are also okay with that as well. Believe us, your soul wants to develop elegant practices of non-grasping and letting go. Your soul wants you to be that beautiful!

Pie-in-the-sky thinking about love

We sometimes get seduced by what we think is love and the feeling we believe we'll receive from love. We sell out for the fantasy, even to the point of tolerating what is not loving, attentive, or caring in a relationship. Our hearts settle, because we are in a love fog, believing that this is, perhaps the best we can do.

And when we're dating someone who we feel isn't great for us, rather than lovingly ending the relationship, fear enters and we think, "What if there's no one after this person who will love me?"

Don't buy into this notion. Wake up! You can do so much better. Keep praying. Keep your standard in the arena of real love. And be honest with what you actually have. Don't enter the love fog. This is exactly why we are writing this book.

When Scotty came along, Shannon began to realize that she was the one being licked! (Hopefully you didn't' skip around in this book and miss the cows!) What a tremendous change in her life! That picture represented a shift to a higher place of expectation for herself, where she decided she couldn't settle for less.

What if you don't now have a soul mate?

You don't have to have a soul mate to have great and lasting love & happy companionship. Just as you don't have to have a million dollars in order to be happy! With love, it's not all or nothing. There are many purposes for which you come together & at different times. But for now, let's discuss soul dating.

How can you position yourself to be more likely to meet the one?

It helps to live within circles of people similar to yourself who are also soul oriented, embracing values, and practicing spirituality. Here are some things you may want to incorporate.

- Seek out those who are heart-minded.
- Seek out those who are open-minded like yourself and who are interested in a relationship of a higher nature.
- Seek out those who are kind, respectful, and who enable you to feel emotionally safe. Get really good at doing this yourself with others.
- Start to love more people around you by identifying their Higher Selves and telling them gently how you are viewing them in this way.
- Practice seeing yourself as a divine Self – immortal and eternal and spiritual – and as one who continues beyond a dying experience.
- View yourself with less criticism and greater love.
- See yourself more as a Higher Self rather than as a human personality, and as one who incarnated to make a difference in the world, to give your love.
- Ask Spirit to guide you.
- Lighten up and be ready to laugh.

If there is no spiritual circle available to you, how can you find someone that is a soul mate or soul mate friend?

This may take a lot of effort, but remember, everyone needs love. Just give it. And when it comes to finding a true soul companion, you'll need to stick your neck out a bit in order to have your spirituality somewhat visible. One thing is for sure, your love will be appreciated by everyone. Your spirituality will help to draw in those who are also on the path like yourself.

You'll find out very quickly how open someone is to a discussion about soul or spirituality. Those who are not open are far more in number than those who are open, so be wise and discerning. You may start by asking your new friend or date, one of the following questions:

- Are you reading any interesting spiritual books? If so, what's the part that most interests you?
- Are you interested in spirituality?
- Do you like watching Oprah's Master classes or Soul Mate Sundays?
- Do you ever rely on your intuition? When was the last time and what did you intuit?
- Do you think about spiritual things? (meaning of life, love, mindfulness, meditation, prayer, self-reflection, the presence of God, angels, yourself as energy, spiritual teachings, metaphysics, or spiritual healing).
- Do you journal?

Whenever the answer is "yes" to any of these, or similar, questions, try to start a discussion. Use follow up questions and let them know that you are also very interested in these subjects. Share something that's important to you from your own studies, perhaps something you are discovering to be true.

Just because someone is reading spiritual books or going to yoga retreats doesn't mean they are living the principles. Be discerning. okay?

Transparency is the road to intimacy and love. But with transparency, there's always the risk that you may not be well received or understood. That's the cost of transparency. And it's well worth it. Keep making gentle efforts. Some will connect. And for those who don't, that's okay too. Just let them go.

Usually, people on a spiritual path are reading many of the same books. These are great topics for discussion.

It is important to engage in spiritual discussions. Use your throat chakra and let it open up and be a voice for what you are learning that is valuable to you.

Notice resistance you may have to sharing in a discussion. What's that about? You've been silent and invisible long enough. Start talking and exposing yourself. There's no way intimacy occurs without it.

In spiritual discussions, we aren't talking about inviting someone's ego with a million opinions, who's a know-it-all or who has to be right. The spiritual path is more about humble discoveries that you are finding through insights and practices.

There's no ego involved with who's right or wrong. It's not a competition. It's merely sharing precious insights or truths and in loving and respectful ways. And no one feels put down. In fact, both partners feel elevated. Do you have an elevating relationship?

We promise, that as you learn to keep the door open for ongoing, sincere, spiritual discussions, it will change you. You and the person you are dating will start to find a deep common thread that wants to weave and fill itself with greater meaning and connection.

It feels so good to share at this level and it is also rare, so you will want to seek out these types of relationships above all others.

These discussions are not intellectual. No one monopolizes or else it's boring and unequal. Remember the talking stick. Each one gets a turn. You may even need to facilitate as you begin a discussion with, "This is such an important subject. Let's each take a turn talking and listening to each other. And, perhaps, afterward, we can reflect back what we think we heard."

Be sure to take a moment to honor each other after each of you has spoken. You may have to be the model of how this is done.

For example, it's possible that the person you are with has revealed something never shared with anyone before this moment. It can create a feeling of great vulnerability, even anxiety.

Thank them and let them know what it meant to you that they shared and, as a result of their sharing, how you now feel more connected to their soul. Share your gratitude when you acknowledge someone's soul. It's their gift to you. Don't take it for granted. You know that these are life's most wonderful moments.

Something happens when you learn to speak from the heart. Your enthusiasm and passion become unlocked! Hello bliss!

Try to suspend your strong doubts about ever meeting the one. Doubts will only make you nervous and afraid. They are a heavy burden that weighs on you and they invade your brightly lit hopes. They aren't part of your soul.

Consider how soul mates come together and often, it's against all odds. It happens anyway. We were over 100 miles apart from each and living in separate cities, unlikely to ever meet.

Yet the soul has a plan for the connection. Enjoy trusting that.

What if you're dating and your heart is racing with hope?

First, are you in harmony with your soul? There's a shift that needs to take place in order for this to occur. Here's your checklist.

- Be true to yourself.
- Speak your truth using kind words and honesty.
- Enjoy giving your gifts of love, sharing, and caring.
- Stay in your high vibration, while quietly releasing all that doesn't belong to you such as negative feelings which distract your soul from shining.
- There are times, though, that negative thoughts or feelings are our information centers that are trying to protect us. In which case, we need to discern the difference.

Once you meet your soul mate, you'll likely feel excited, even though it may not yet be confirmed that this is your soul mate. Begin right then, bringing your Higher Self to the relationship. We recommend you practice the standard and quality of soul mate love from the start of a strong soulful attraction, even if you haven't determined that this is the one.

Begin by establishing a standard of ongoing harmony. It's absolutely essential to all relationships. This shouldn't compromise who you are. It's merely an effort to bring peace as you come into an understanding of this new special person in your life. We never could understand why couples with new budding love risk it all and begin to argue when they hardly know each other!

Also try to be in harmony with the rate that the relationship is progressing. Let the relationship find a natural flow, getting together as it's comfortable for you both, even though one of you may want to go faster. It's hard, when you're excited, to be calm, but it's important to the progression of the relationship so it has a chance to grow.

At the beginning of the relationship, and as you discover that you are intensely enjoying time with your mate, and you want even more time together, fear may push you to know if this is the one. Or fear could cause you to create an uncomfortable demand on your mate.

This is a time where you especially want to maintain the standard of harmony, respect, and non-pushiness. See how you are already starting to set the bar higher because you are rising to practice the standard of soul mate love?

It's understandable that, as the relationship develops into something wonderful, that feelings of budding love can feel intense. After all, you've waited so long, and this could be the one, and what if it doesn't work out! Yikes!

This is a time, however, to recognize that your feelings of uneasiness are probably normal. It's also a time to try and calm down and set aside the fear.

Fear is a wrecker. Either this is the one or it isn't. If it is, you'll come to know in the right time and way. Be patient and don't push. Try to be strong and honorable to respect the "getting to know you" period which you both need. And, for heaven's sake, enjoy the dating period!

As you get to know each other, be ready to share your feelings, to deepen your understanding and compassion, and make efforts to identify their soul. Be prepared, if you can, to spend happy times together - without games, manipulation, pressure, stress, or arguing. You are setting the stage to practice soul mate love. This is where it begins.

We look back on our dating period with immediate smiles. We had so much fun getting to know each other! Our times spent together were focused on ourselves, laughing, playing, and enjoying each other. We never argued or pushed, though we each had our fears, of course.

When we were dating, Shannon was doubtful and distrusting of her judgment, having come out of a long, marriage, full of disappointments.

So, when Scott told her, early on, that he was in love with her and wanted to marry her, she wasn't at all sure of her feelings due to so many layers of defenses built up from being wounded by the marriage. She couldn't sort through the maze at that early time. There were still emotions of distrust that she was clearing.

At one time, Scott lovingly told her that he understood and accepted if she didn't feel the same way or wasn't' sure of her love for him. '

He gently shared that he didn't want to be with someone unless they loved him equally. This wasn't a manipulation to push her towards a decision. And it wasn't an ultimatum. It was the honesty of his heart. No games. No hurt feelings. Just the truth. It was information. We were getting to know each other souls.

We kept dating and acted as mature adults, realizing that it may not work out. We just didn't yet know. Time would tell. And, yes, we were very excited and nervous. We pressed on!

Shannon was deeply impressed with his independence and non-clinging, unconditional love. It began healing her of the wounds as she felt the energy field he was offering her of emotional freedom, without burden or pressure from his need to know.

His words were genuine. It was dignified. She admired him. She found herself enormously attracted to him and it began to open her heart as fear began to melt. She began to realize our growing, deep connection. As a woman, she felt immensely respected. And it meant a lot.

She needed a zero-pressure approach. She couldn't push herself to feel trust or love, though she sensed it. The heart has its own timing. During this period, Scott's respect towards her emotional block sent volumes of loving messages to her heart. Note to soul mates: mutual respect is always paramount in soul mate love.

When we were first dating, we didn't know where our journey of love was taking us. We knew, however, that what we were experiencing was like nothing either of us had ever known or heard about. We were in awe of the feelings of how great our love felt and the happiness it was bringing to each of us.

We were immensely excited that, on top of that, we had spirituality in common, which multiplied our love to the moon and back.

But we hadn't yet walked the path of our love. We had no idea it would develop as it has to a powerful journey of spiritual awakening.

We recognize that there are couples who consider themselves to be soul mates, but they don't consider themselves to be on a spiritual journey. And these soul mates haven't yet found a lot of words to describe each other's wonderfulness. Perhaps they don't feel a need to. They are so filled by each other's love and enjoyment that that is enough. And they find that this love is lasting through the years and deepens them with shared interests and experiences meaningful to each of them. They are, in short, very happy and deeply in love.

We celebrate these soul mate couples! The world needs more of them!

And while it is absolutely wonderful that they share their love at such deep levels, there is so much more waiting for them if and when they decide to go higher.

When two people recognize themselves as souls who have found each other, and they embark on a journey for their souls to soar and awaken, this is the beauty that awaits soul mates.

We encourage you to take the plunge and go for the biggest soul event you can imagine! Become an awakened soul mate!

As your journey evolves deeper into soul mate love, here's another soul secret: As you become more and more talented at soul talk, you will find more and more soul mate love.

Are you ready to learn more about soul talk?

Chapter 6

Soul Talk

Soul mate love thrives on soul talk. It not only thrives on soul talk, it explodes into the highest dimensions of soul love.

Most people, however, are too afraid to initiate soul talk or never learned how.

Let's reason this through. You want a soul mate, yes? You'd like to meet someone who expresses the qualities of soul we've been discussing in this book, yes? You'd like for your soul mate to experience your soul, yes?

The key connection in all these desires is soul visibility. How can you meet your soul mate, or develop soul mate love, while your own soul is hidden?

We want to encourage you to step into your soul. Begin to express it. Let your soul light be evident. Your soul mate needs to see your light to find you. And you need to see evidence of your own light in order for your soul to become even more awakened.

The best way to do this is to be generously loving – to everyone - as a soul.

Some people light up only when they think someone might be the one, or might be important to them. They reserve their love exclusively for "the one." Limiting your soul light to only one or a few has a way of diminishing your own soul light within. You can lose touch with your soul self.

Soul love is inclusive. It needs to love, to radiate, to bless, to bring joy to others. This is a huge secret for finding your soul mate.

Start loving everyone. Generously offer your sweet, loving smiles. Not only will the world feel more love from you, but you will discover yourself as a true love being, a genuine soul lover. The effect of this life style – really a love style – is incredible.

Scott's dad was a role model to him of this loving style. Whenever he went into a store, he'd talk to the cashier as though the person was his best friend. The same at restaurants, on the street, or with Scott's friends. His dad was so good at building love connections that even when Scott, in high school, broke up with a girlfriend, his Dad was still friends with her.

Interestingly, Scott's dad was of the generation where men didn't talk much, and Scott often wishes he had been able to have more intimate dialogue with his dad. But his example of open kindness stuck with Scott.

It's probably one reason Scott is so comfortable with soul talk.

If you tend towards being an introvert, we encourage you to come forth where more love awaits you!

An example of Scott's soul talk

When I'm having lunch with Shannon at one of our soul lunches, my heart wants to know what's in her heart, but first I take a soul reading, basically letting my love tune into her soul.

Is she happy and free? Is something bothering her? Is she down? Is she eager to share something with me? Is she distracted? Does she need lifting up?

By taking the love temperature, I'm allowing my soul to find the best path into her heart. My goal is for her to feel deeply loved.

If she's happy and free, I might say, "Sweetie, you seem very happy. Tell me about that," and then just be quiet while she ponders my question. A soul-tuned question like this can trigger someone to feel the freedom to fully unpack what's in their heart.

If Shannon seems concerned, I might say, "Sweetie, what's going on in your heart?" and then listen quietly to what she wishes to share. The words may come out slowly as she gets in touch with herself to check in.

This is how the soul talks – and listens.

Because I'm not afraid to speak in soul language, my heart is free to develop the most sumptuous questions. One of my current favorites is to ask Shannon, "If there is one thing your soul would like me to know right now, what would that be?"

Here's a soul love insight. I've been married to Shannon for 25 years and we spend an amazing amount of time together as soul mates, so you'd think, wouldn't you, that I would already know the answer to that question, right?

Absolutely wrong. As soul beings, our hearts are in constant motion. We are evolving in Spirit. And we are wrestling with the human condition in all its daily variations. A soul question breaks through the barrier of separation to create deep heart unity.

Love is continuously surprising. Shannon's answers surprise me, delight me, help me to more closely understand her and what she is experiencing, or inform me that I need to tune in more, or give more love.

Soul talk while dating

Can you have soul talk when you first meet someone or you're on an early date?

You sure can. Remember, what if this person might actually be your soul mate? Would you like him or her to see your soul – or do you plan to keep it hidden & miss out on an opportunity for soul mate love?

But here's an even deeper insight into soul mate love. Who cares if this is your soul mate. Don't you want this relationship, no matter what it is destined to be, to be anchored in soul rather than love fog? Don't you want the real thing – in all your relationships?

If your date disappears because you show your soul, you've done an immense favor to your love life. You have instantly created more open space for true soul love by recognizing what doesn't belong in your soul-inspired life.

Here is an easy, non-threatening (to you or your date) love question, "What are you most passionate about?"

That beautiful soul question leaves the door wide open for the other person to go shallow or go deep, and it's an invitation to have easy love talk that focuses on soul.

At one of our workshops, a wife arrived for the morning session, but her husband arrived several hours later. Scott wanted him to ease into the workshop without stress, and asked him, outside the room, "What are you most passionate about?" He said, "Intimacy." Scott really laughed at that and said, you're totally up to speed, head on in.

When Scott later brought this up to the group, his wife said to her husband, "Really? That's what your most passionate about? Is that why you ask me so many questions?" The group really laughed at that. And so did they.

But here's the insight. This couple had been married many years and deeply loved each other. But their soul talk wasn't out in the open. With one love question by Scott, this became evident to both of them.

After this discovery, their intimacy increased dramatically. She now realized that his soul yearned for deeper connection with her. And she accepted. Once his soul's visibility became more apparent to them both, it took them forward into greater soulmate love.

It may feel scary to ask a love question, even an easy one. But aren't you reading this book so you can take your love life into the arena of soul mate love?

You just can't have soul mate love without soul. You can have love, even wonderful love, but you can't experience soul mate love without soul. That makes sense, doesn't it?

This is really good news. This clears the path. Your heart can now accept that you want the real thing and for that, your soul needs to come out of hiding and be visible so you can love and be loved at a soul level.

Sometimes, when it comes time to draw closer to someone, we have reluctance because we intuitively feel emotionally unsafe. Pay attention to this always. Be self-protective and don't open a door that you already know may not go well for you.

But at other times, when you are with someone who you feel emotionally safe with, and you want to draw closer, the fastest way to eliminate shyness or fear in asking soul questions is to let go of ego and anything that would prevent you from speaking up and initiating soul talk – fear, lack of courage, basic discomfort, or reluctance.

Just because you've never dared to create this level of intimacy doesn't mean you can't learn. Step outside your comfort zone. Allow yourself to make some mistakes. It's worth it!

Rather than dwelling on how hesitant you feel, or how the other person will feel, allow yourself the soul freedom to be the presence of love. Let love do the asking. You be the vehicle. Let love drive.

A soul question from us to you

Before we continue talking to you in this book, we have a soul question for you. "What does your soul most want you to know & do right now?"

Take a quiet moment and think about that. Our love is with you even though we are not physically present. Our souls are resonating with your soul.

More soul-opening questions

There's no end to the variety of soul questions you can ask. Let your soul come up with your own phrasing. This is not intellectual. Listen to your soul and let your soul dream up the questions. Here are some soul questions we love asking:

- What's going on in your heart right now?
- What's most on your mind?
- What are you most learning in your life right now?
- What is thrilling your soul the most at this moment of your life?
- What are you not talking about because no one is asking?
- What's going on deep within your soul?
- What are you most feeling about your life right now?

See? Soul mates are constantly checking in, drawing close, learning, and discovering about each other. This brings joy, intimacy, discovery, self-expression, expansion, and greater self-realization!

Wouldn't you want to know about your greater self? Your Higher Self - what it looks like and how it characterizes you?

There are hidden clues that are well worth the search since they lead to indescribable happiness. Is it any wonder that Plato and Socrates as well as other master philosophers through the ages, gave so much weight to the discussion and importance of the soul?

The arc of our love

One night, during his private reflection time, Scott thought to himself: "I feel inspired to define my relationship with Shannon through something artistic, rather than words." Here's the story in Scott's words:

I'm not much of an artist, but I pulled out my ipad and drew this simple picture of two lines overlapping and on a constant upward arc.

To me, this perfectly defines our soul mate love. I nicknamed it "The arc of our love" and couldn't wait to share it with Shannon.

Here's what's interesting. Of course, we've had ups and downs in our individual lives. Jobs have changed. Careers have changed. Relationships have changed. Our life chart, from that perspective, would look like the continuous rise and fall of the stock market.

But our soul love transcends those ups and downs. Life challenges bring us closer together – and elevate us, because, with each negative turn of events, we turn to soul for higher answers.

That's the ecstasy of our soul mate love. It's a line of constant upward movement – together. This simple drawing perfectly defines our love & life together.

This paralleling, upward movement together represents our path of ascension – rising in the evolution of our Higher Selves.

We're all on a path of ascension, whether we know it or not. Every challenge in your life creates an opportunity to rise higher. Think back on your life. Would you like to be today who you were ten years ago? Not likely. You've advanced. We're all on a path of ascension.

In soul mate love, you get the opportunity to be on that path of ascension together. This is exhilarating to the soul.

We discussed this drawing over lunch the next day – the entire lunch. That's what we do. This is a perfect example of "Soul Talk" in action. When one of us gets inspired by soul, we share it and then discuss it from lots of angles.

Embedded in this drawing is unity. Scotty has a way of crossing boundaries, interconnecting. It's what his yellow grid does as a soul.

At lunch, we both realized that the upward curve would definitely not be as steep if we didn't have each other. We constantly help each other evolve in our understanding of soul.

And that word "evolve" is a big one for soul mate love. Nothing stays static. Change is the nature of life.

Just so, no love relationship, even the very best, stays static. In our soul mate love, we are constantly evolving. We know that, and we use our constant "soul talk" time to help each other rise on that path of ascension.

If you were a little bird listening in to our lunch, you would see the two of us laughing, sharing ideas, debating, disagreeing from time to time without any anger, listening, laughing more, & relishing our time together. We often even take notes!

As a result of the lunch, Shannon noted with great joy that she was meeting Scott's Higher Self in a powerful way as we discussed the diagram of our evolution together. She noted how much we needed each other to reach our soul potential.

We both know how difficult it is to identify one's Higher Self and then try to bring that Higher Self into 3D "normal" living. We talk about this a lot – especially since the 3D human world throws us all so many constant challenges that can trip up our happiness.

Scott noted that these constant 3D challenges – in work, relationships, even politics – can quickly create fear, anger, doubt, and frustration. Yet, our response to these conditions is always a choice.

We can choose to respond as our Higher Self, our Soul Self.

Or we can sink into the quicksand of negative emotions.

Truthfully, it usually doesn't feel like we have a choice, but that's the importance of staying focused on soul.

Whenever you are thinking out from your Soul Self, it becomes clear that you always have the choice to respond as your Higher Self.

Moving through tough and dark waters together is one of the most wonderful gifts to our soul mate love. We help each other rise.

When one of us is down, the other doesn't sink down too. We seek to comfort each other, inspire each other, and rise higher – to the place we know we belong.

At this lunch, Scott said, "I think I live in soul space about 50% of the time and in the fear and doubt from the 3D world 50%. I'd like it be 80% soul space in my life." Shannon greatly appreciated knowing his insight about himself. It is through such honest sharing that we grapple our way higher.

Through our constant "soul talk," we feel we are helping each other cross new frontiers in soul space. This creates an enormous bond of love united in soul.

So, all of that is just one evening diagram of love and one lunch discussion in our lives, but that's how soul talk unfolds.

Not all our conversations are "soul talk." As any two people in a relationship, we have lots of discussions of challenges, hopes, relationships, family, work, and arrangements.

Yet we probably average about 65% of our talk time together as "soul talk." Can you imagine how good that feels!

Don't think that's impossible for you. Think of that more as a real possibility and something you deserve in your life. Soul talk breeds more soul love. And remember, you don't have to have a soul mate yet to have soul talk. You can get your "soul talk" polished every day by using it with people all around your life.

We hope you will look for opportunities for soulful discussions either with a special friend, a family member, with a date, or within a group.

Some of the New Thought churches have wonderful spiritual book discussions. Out of these come more friends and opportunities to share and be together.

Buddhists have sangha communities where they meditate and listen to teacher's talks together. It's a wonderful experience to be within a like-minded group learning deeper things and awakening to the same things that you are.

You will discover that, as you dwell on the subject of soul, you will want more. You will discover deeper parts which you long for and which long to be discovered and brought out. It's healing.

The more that you practice soul talk, the more you improve, and the percentage of time you spend in soul increases dramatically. There's not much better preparation than that for attracting a soul mate.

But that doesn't even have to be your focus. Let your life flow with "soul talk" so that you can be inspired and stay in the space of your Higher Self.

People around you will feel your inspired energy. They will want to be with you. They will be attracted to you.

And you will be constantly rising in soul. Your language will become more refined in love. Your motives will rise more into soul. Others will connect more easily with you.

Isn't this the love you want? It's a way of life – walking through life as your Soul Self. And as you look at your life through the lens of soul pods, you will find even more opportunities for soul talk – and soul relationships. Let's talk about soul pods.

Chapter 7

Soul Pods

Soul pods share a lot in common with soul mate relationships. They bring together two or more souls in order to serve a higher purpose.

Soul pods are attracted through each other's Higher Self. They also serve to elevate, inspire, and increase the spiritual power of the Higher Selves involved. They generally occur naturally.

You can't force a soul pod relationship. But maybe as you read on, you'll recognize yourself in one of these pods.

They may be short term or long term, depending on their common purpose. Some soul pods occur in families and may be long term. Others may occur within a time frame where there is something to be accomplished together and, once the purpose has ended, pod members may go their separate ways.

However, once you have come together with any member of your pod, you are forever bonded in an unforgettable experience in the human realm. No one will easily forget it. And you will always look back with a smile reflecting on the extraordinary feeling, operating within your pod, whether it's with one other person or many.

Soul pods activate the soul, or Higher Self. Generally, because of the spiritual depth operating within a soul pod, it can bring great happiness and joy. Each one finds value at this level of higher-purposed relationships, especially when there's less ego and more soul expressed. These offer opportunities for the soul's greater spiritual evolution.

They operate optimally when they develop the same skills as soul mates. Look for one or more of these qualities in a soul pod:

- Loving.
- Compassionate.
- Cooperating, harmonious, and helpful.
- Mutually engaged in higher service or a noble purpose.
- Empowering to others.
- Passionate about what they are doing and doing it with excellence.
- Forgiving.
- Treating each other with mutual respect and equality.
- Supportive to the whole and perhaps even protective.
- Feeling part of something bigger than themselves.

A soul pod nurtures the Higher Self. It brings out our best.

Examples of soul pods

We have friends and family members who are deeply spiritual and loving. We recognize each other's souls. We adore them! Whenever we're together, we often have deep spiritual discussions. Sometimes we share insights or support for whatever any of us is going through, and our love lingers long afterward with prayers, extended love, and connection. We laugh a lot too.

There's something powerful that occurs when you rise to witness another's soul, above and beyond everyday circumstances. This reminder of who you are is a gift beyond all proportions and it is always welcomed.

Do you have any of these soul pod connections?

During the many years Shannon was a professional spiritual healer, she experienced innumerable soul pods, since both her soul, as well as her clients, were fully engaged for their healing purposes.

Great depths and heights of love and healing came out of those powerful sessions as they were guided during the awakened states of healing. Outcomes are amazing whenever the soul is fully engaged. The healing pods, and what they shared, will remain in her heart forever.

Other examples of soul pods

There's a family close to us who has an uncanny closeness as a soul pod. The two parents raised their kids with great mindfulness towards their spiritual teachings and towards becoming loving people.

These are parents who also lived and modeled it to their children, even disciplining with tenderness and respectfulness. While the parents were greatly involved with raising their kids, they also carried a tremendously tender love for them.

Even after their kids became adults, they have still shared a great deal of love, laughter, and spiritual discussions about life. How fortunate they are to have so much in common and to enjoy sitting around, just being together.

Best friends are often soul mate pods. Usually with fun and mutual interests and caring, through deep discussions where each feels emotionally safe, supported, and listened to, love pours in. A deep bond follows.

Just because someone calls themselves a best friend doesn't necessarily mean that they are soul mate companions or in a soul pod with you.

If there is competitiveness, jealousy, dishonesty and such, of course, it's not soul mate love quality. Go for the highest qualities in a friend. You will each grow and create more love and expansion for each other and hopefully, be of soul pod quality, where you are mutually supportive of each other's hopes, dreams, and lives. No judgments!

We have a friend, who, for years, has had a passion to organize house builds for families in Mexico without homes. She eventually bought a truck and loaded it each week with goods that people generously donated.

She crosses the border and works with a church to distribute the items. This has evolved to a bigger distribution where she contacted contractors who dropped off windows, cabinets, doors, and other things that were being discarded during remodels. She even had to buy a bigger truck for her weekly trek!

Kathy named her organization Casas de Luz. Houses of Light. Her great compassion turned her into a humanitarian to these folks in Mexico. Her home building projects spilled over to a community center and she often drops off items for the orphanage. She and her group recently completed building a new church for them.

Whatever she gives to these people is more than paid back to her by their gratitude.

This is a good example of a soul pod, not just with those receiving the homes but the bond of love of those on the building teams. And Kathy as their leader.

Wherever you are following your soul's calling, uniting with others in service and with heart invested, you are involved with your soul pod. It's especially happy and fulfilling when its received by the other party with gratitude and appreciation. Then it becomes bigger than just one soul in service.

Mother Theresa and the nuns in her order were definitely a soul pod to dying souls so that they could die with dignity and love.

Our primary care doctor, Dr. Luigi Simone, runs an amazing soul pod. From the time they answer the phone, you feel the love and care.

We have often been surprised at the depth of care Shannon's parents received, and for years through their nineties, all led by Dr. Luigi Simone and his outstanding health care group at Scripps Medical in San Diego. We were always met by love, listening attention, consideration, and taken the extra mile to discuss ever changing new health conditions they faced (what a learning curve!). And it always felt as though we were the only patients he had. We couldn't have been more grateful!

During years of caregiving to her parents, Shannon was often at the ER and spent a great deal of time at the hospital with one or the other parent. She must have worked with dozens of doctors and maybe hundreds of nurses and technicians. She often asked them to tell her the story of what led them to health care. And with little exception, it was a calling. Hello soul pod! Many soul pods come together in the health field.

Shannon's dad played golf every week and for all his life. Little did she know that it was a soul pod!

Once, when he was deathly ill in the hospital, she and her mom spent the morning by his side. There were tears as the doctor shared his grave prognosis. Her Dad had hardly opened his eyes in weeks. Shannon and her Mom sat there together, next to her dad, often crying that morning as the gravity of the situation sank in.

One of his golf buddies called and said they would like to come by that afternoon. We explained that he was unconscious but to please come anyway.

Shannon and her mom had a big surprise as a result of the golf buddies' visit. About seven of them stood around his bed. Their pastor was also present and he decided to lead them in the Lord's Prayer.

As the men's voices sounded the words, her dad began to repeat the prayer along with them. And not in a soft voice, but a booming voice, as though he were being called back from the dead! After that day, he improved rapidly. Never underestimate the power of a soul pod!

By following your heart, you can find a soul pod that speaks to your heart and that fulfills something within you as a giving channel that nothing else can. It will fill you and cause you to live from your higher place of heart and soul.

Here's another type of soul pod.

Shannon's brother, Jed, and his wife, Pam, were invested in their soul's passion during the years that they lived along a trout river in Arkansas. They managed their son's fishing store. It was the hang out for fishermen, who loved coming to the store where coffee was served and sometimes even Pam's chili.

Her brother was passionate about trout fishing and was also a river guide. He made it his business to know where the fish were each day, which was an ongoing hot topic of discussion. This often led to his being on the local radio and even writing books about the Little Red River. Many united around the Little Red.

They were also a part of a passionate group who loved the river and the nature experience. They called themselves the River Rats and gathered monthly to clear trash from the river banks and surrounding area. It gave their lives great meaning to be connected to nature and to a group who was equally passionate about the river.

Many churches are soul pods because members can share an intimate spiritual experience together, whether through group prayer, song, sermon, or church gatherings and being in service for a common cause.

Other institutions, less church-like, such as the Agape Center for Spiritual Living in Los Angeles, have broken away from the traditional "church" experience and are also soul pods. Agape's name, for example, identifies spiritual living - and love - as the glue that motivates their soul pod.

And guess what? Their pastor and his talented musician wife – Dr. Michael Beckwith and Ricki Buyers – are amazing, true soul mates!

Today, there are thousands of people who identify themselves as "spiritual, but not religious." That's also a soul pod.

You couldn't personally know all the people in that expansive soul pod, but you may be part of it.

You may watch Oprah and her "Super Soul Sunday" shows. That's definitely a soul pod. And speaking of Oprah, she and Gayle are a soul pod!

We have a very important soul pod with our grandson, Atti (short for Atticus). In fact, Shannon met him before he was born!

A few years before his birth, Shannon had been gardening in the backyard, and she became aware of an energy being. He arrived out of nowhere. While she was in the garden one day, suddenly she was aware of a little blonde boy who was running past her with such joy that it was almost unimaginable. He was so overjoyed and laughing that his feet barely touched the ground as he ran past her. It brought a great smile to her heart.

She had never before had such a psychic experience.

At another time, in about the same place, he appeared again and in the same way. As he ran past her, he reminded her of an over-the-top joy that was amazing! By this time, Shannon had been thinking of him, and had even given him a name, Dave. And she thought, that since he loved playing in her back yard, he might like something to play with.

She bought him a lightweight metal gate that opened and closed. And she mounted it on the fence. After that, she didn't sense him again, but she continued to be inspired by this little boy's great joy.

About a year passed. One day, when Shannon was walking from the back yard to the front, she strongly sensed his joyful presence once again. She was overjoyed that he was still with her, expressing his great delight. His presence was tremendously uplifting.

Within a couple years, Shannon's daughter, Kaia, gave birth to a son. Even before he turned one, everyone began to notice he had a sense of humor.

This increased dramatically as he grew. One day, when he was just two or so, as he ran past Shannon, he was laughing and so joyful that his feet barely touched the ground. It was Dave! Clearly recognizable to her senses, but this time he had entered the 3D human experience and brought his incredible joy with him!

Throughout his toddler years, Shannon spent a great deal of time with him and often all three of us spent wonderful times laughing and playing. He's really funny and he learned quickly what made us all laugh, creating immense joy among us.

One thing characteristic of Atti is that whenever he laughs or tries to make us laugh (which is a constant), he always makes eye contact. It creates a feeling of immediate connection and adds a soul dimension to the shared laughter.

Stories of his humor are always at the top of our family discussions as we all laugh together. There have been many times where we three have spent long hours together playing funny games, acting silly, teasing, telling jokes, and laughing our heads off.

The many times we have spent together have left an indelible mark on our hearts and souls, forever.

Even corporations are broadening the highway for soul pods, as they make efforts at making the work place more meaningful. Many are incorporating spiritual practices, offering a place to meditate or relax, emphasizing mindfulness and yoga, treating employees as though their needs matter, while valuing their customers.

Some companies have identified their values by creating a mission statement and developing a culture to make the work place more meaningful and supportive to their employees' mental, emotional, and spiritual well-being.

When it is successful, these companies are creating a soulful environment where it's safe and even encouraged to become more of who you really are – and to express it. This, in turn, causes soul visibility, which makes it easier for people to connect with members of their soul pod, whether it's with one person or a group, or even many groups.

Look around you. You'll start to notice soul pods. As you do, it will increase your awareness and open you to drawing closer to your own soul pods.

The rule of thumb is to follow your heart when it comes to attracting or discovering your soul pod.

Often, out of a soul pod will come soul mates, destined to be together, like us.

We met each other by being part of a soul pod that was creating a love workshop for teens. We had never met before joining that soul pod and we would never have met without being part of that soul pod together.

Chapter 8

Honoring
Soul

At the heart of our soul mate love practice is honoring. This has evolved our love to wonderful places!

Just watch as your soul mate is having a hard day and you sit down and share what you most love about them. And when you do it with generosity, love, and passion, your soul mate will absolutely light up and be lifted right out of their gloom and darkness. It helps enormously! This is what soul mates do! Practice makes perfect.

The nuts and bolts of soul mate love come from the heart when you are using words to generously express your appreciation and gratitude. And, it needs to be specific. Rather than, "You are so wonderful. I love you so much!" chances are your soul mate has already heard that a million times (hopefully!) from you.

It's far more meaningful when you are specific, telling your soul mate what it is about them that you appreciate so much. Hopefully it isn't always the same thing and you're noticing other additional things as the relationship unfolds.

"Honey, do you know what I love most about you right now?"

Who in this room wouldn't stop anything they're doing and listen up?

That's very meaningful information and it actually nurtures the heart, causing it to expand with love. It creates wonderful, blissful feelings from the heart. Isn't that what you want your soul mate to feel? And yourself to feel? This is honoring.

You want something as beautiful as soul mate love? Then you've got to be beautiful and up your game. Just do it. Step across the line of discomfort that you've avoided so long and step into your greater self. It's a tall order but this is soul mate love. You can do this!

We love honoring each other at the highest level, which also raises both our vibrations to higher levels. It creates an energy field of love that we both can appreciate.

Soul honoring creates great conversations! This is soul mate love and it is noble.

It's not coming from judging. We carefully avoid judging as it closes the heart. Acknowledging comes from a genuine appreciation and love for the advancements you have bothered to notice from your love mate who is pouring out their heart towards making a good life for you and themselves! And when you comment on what you are noticing, it means the world.

With soul mate love, the generosity of love, caring, and giving are offered continually and felt as a bulwark. It has to be equally given and received. This equality is essential to harmony and balance in the relationship, which, in turn, offer us a better life.

Within our relationship, there's a constant waterfall flowing from our hearts with regular attention towards each other's advancements.

Sometimes, the acknowledgment will come from a recent hardship overcome and what qualities and skills one of us has noticed it brought forth in our soul mate in order to deal with it.

Other times, the acknowledgment comes from immense gratitude for being so fortunate as to have our soul mate to share our life with!

With the temporary nature and uncertainty of life, we take nothing for granted. This brings us so much love and joy from our soul mate love. Be generous with praise and with love. Without generosity, you won't be in soul mate love. It's that simple.

The time to enjoy and express your appreciation is now.

Please do this often and do it thoroughly. You can even begin by saying, "I'd like to take a moment to acknowledge you. I have no idea what I am going to say, but I want to make some sacred space to love you and find words that express what I am feeling and how much I care."

It would be powerful to incorporate this practice regularly. The more you practice, the better you get and the bigger the love grows. We promise!

Let us just say here that it's more than offering compliments. That's not the goal. Acknowledgment is recognition of the worth and value of another soul. It's part of that soul's awakening and adds immensely to it.

By reflecting back what you notice to be part of your soul mate's character, their intrinsic qualities or essence, their energy field, offering feedback on how you see them in their light, you are lifting an epic curtain that is life changing and potentially gigantic for their greater happiness.

It carries ultimate meaning and potential. Do you know how much we all crave this? And yet how rare it is?

This is the love that feeds our souls. Learning how you are being perceived in your best light is a gift of inestimable value.

Equality

In soul mate love there are not roles of one being a giver and the other acting as a receiver. That would foster selfishness, the opposite of love. It just doesn't work.

Both mates need to be ongoing generous givers to each other.

And, it doesn't make sense to do your acknowledgment half way. Why hold back? Love doesn't act this way. The bigger your acknowledgment, the bigger the field of love you create around you both. The appreciation that comes back is enormous! Your generosity billows into your becoming magnanimous. What a great, big-hearted feeling that is! And it changes you to becoming a person of great magnanimity. Beautiful!

Who else is going to acknowledge your soul mate in that way! People just don't go around doing this kind of thing, unfortunately. If your soul mate and you are going to get this kind of appreciation, acknowledgment, and love, it's going to have to come from you. You two are about soul mate love, right? This is how soul mate love acts.

Your soul requires a soul mate who is just as generous as you in caring, patience, restraint, and all the gifts of soul's love. Don't settle for less.

This is your soul we are discussing! It's important! And for God's sake, don't pretend you have soul mate love when you don't. If you need to complain, be loving and use kind speech. You must speak up when it isn't right. Your soul mate needs to know and understand how you are.

Don't make excuses for your soul mate's unaddressed bad temper, closed heart, apathy, or excuses for being uncomfortable talking about love, sharing things from the heart, or their growth or lack of it. These are not the actions of a soul mate, and everyone knows it.

These do not produce soul mate love.

Living in the hope that your mate will someday change is not facing the reality. It is actually enabling your mate to back off the responsibility of soul duties to you. We need both parties engaged in order for our hearts to sing and be in the field of soul mate love.

Both hearts become sweeter and grander through the art of acknowledgment. Even children can learn it, and the earlier in life, the better. Your soul thrives on acknowledging others and being acknowledged yourself. Get good at this. You can change a life in less than one minute of generous, waterfall acknowledgement!

Let's take it a step higher. Rather than just commenting and acknowledging or praising your mate on their wonderful human qualities, offer recognition and acknowledgment and praise of their soul. Who does that? Soul mates do!

Soul mates treat each other as their number one priority. Your soul mate is that important. Making your soul mate less important than your job or other activities won't enable you to reach the heights of soul mate love.

Let us interrupt your reading for a moment and ask you to pull back, create space, and ask yourself if you are receiving all this as possible for yourself? Or, are you piling up doubts?

Let us assure you that you are born to love and be loved! Even though you may have suffered some hard knocks (we all have), your desire for soul mate love is the desire of your soul. This is coming from a place within that knows. Let it guide you. Suspend your doubt and press on with an open heart.

We've spent years identifying each other's souls

What you will read in this book about our relationship defies description. We have an extraordinary relationship and we decided not to hold back any of the description of its amazing sweetness and what ways we relate which most makes our hearts sing.

One of those most precious things that we do and have done for 25 years, which accounts for the tremendous love we share and even bliss, is in the all-out discovery of each other's souls.

To discover your soul mate's soul is the biggest gift you can give. It opens a doorway to all love's treasures and it creates out-of-this world bliss. Love's infinite nature becomes alive within your heart.

We have called ourselves the happiest couple in the universe and that's why!

There was a lot taking place during our dating period as we were learning about each other while greatly enjoying each other. Scott often drove from San Diego to L.A. where Shannon lived and where we spent extended weekends together. Nearly always, during those 3-day periods, we would come up with additional ways of identifying each other in terms of spiritual qualities. Little did we know that we were discovering each other's souls.

In Shannon's professional healing practice, she found that healings came about more powerfully as she identified a client's soul. Accuracy was important. She loved the process of this insight as she felt it brought her closer to view the person's innate identity and condition as a divine being. It was powerful to develop healings in her clients lives, even with their health.

Early on, Shannon decided to make it her mission to see Scotty's soul become visible. She had a profound intuition about Scott's powerful spirituality, which was not as obvious to Scott, because he was somewhat shy.

Every time she caught another glimpse, she made a mental note and shared it with him, celebrating. This was encouraging to him and he gained confidence to reveal more and more of himself. What an uncovering! It brought us into amazing intimacy! And it began to change us both, taking us to a far higher place than we'd ever been.

Although this was a natural course in our dating, it took on a life of its own without our knowing that what we were doing was leading to powerful spiritual vision and intuition and greater enlightenment for each of us, as well as the identification of us as soul mates! It was a path of its own.

We often asked each other what top four things we most liked about each other. Shannon consistently identified Scott as kind, unifying, loving, and spiritual. These represented his patterns of behavior most obvious to her and ones which she treasured. And Scott most often identified Shannon as: healing, spiritual, loving, and full of joy.

These weren't fluffy words. They were sufficiently evident within our lives that the identification was obvious and easy to recognize as true. These are areas that most couples never enter. It's truly sacred territory and it vastly increases your field of love and your capacity to love.

The qualities we were identifying represented the repeating patterns which each of us loved about the other and counted on. We were filled with appreciation for each other as we discovered the lovingkindness we shared.

We had entered a practice, without knowing, of how to grow soul mate love. Our love grew in this fertile ground of identifying each other's top qualities which really, in essence, was honoring each other's souls.

This pattern of identifying each other's souls and honoring these qualities became a regular habit and has remained so for 25 years!

There's been a running list on each other's characteristics since we started dating. In fact, after a few months of dating, it was Shannon's birthday. Scott gave her a book naming the top 50 things he most loved about her!

Here are a few of the 50 things:

- She is my best and most wonderful friend.
- Her support is stronger than the entire Japanese nation of Sumo wrestlers!
- She dances with delight and freedom.
- She speaks with wonderful, nurturing, healing love to the whole world.
- Her healing treatments lift me to heights of glorious awareness never before imagined.
- She expresses the joy and freedom of soul.
- She puts her arm around my neck when we walk.
- She teases me unmercifully.
- She is a full time happy healer supporting the highest post of service in the universe.
- She understands equality, believes in it, and seeks to live it.
- She loves to race me!
- She has the courage to be completely honest with me.

- She laughs and laughs and laughs. What a joy!
- She is real.
- She loves me wonderfully and unconditionally!

You can see by this sampling, how fun and gushing with love it was – as well as deeply honoring. But it also reveals some of Shannon's soul qualities beginning to be recognized by Scotty – loving, supportive, caring, nurturing, equality, joyful, light hearted, healing, honest. This is how it starts.

By the way, before you start comparing yourself to the list, remember, this is Scotty's view of Shannon. It's the view of someone who loves her. He saw her through love's eyes. When someone sees you through love's eyes, your list will also be extraordinary.

Letting in more soul light

With so much love to appreciate, we are still dwelling in a human experience. And, it seems like there's always something that isn't going just right. This is where we each have a personal spiritual practice in order to address the problems. This leads us to deepen our love for each other as we share these practices during our ups and downs.

At bedtime, Scotty spends time making a list of things bothering him, which have been on his mind. He briefly addresses each one of the items, bringing in positive images and visions of the highest solutions, bringing light into these dark areas of his consciousness.

And Shannon does this as well. She also lists the looming problems and negative feelings going on within her. (There's always something!) And each negative item receives a deluge of light and prayer. Much of her journaling consists of asking for divine guidance and writing down the guidance as she receives it. She lives by this.

These, sometimes, become our breakfast conversations. They reveal what things are on our mind. They connect us intimately. They are often inspiring, giving insight on how we each tackle the human experience with divine guidance. This is a subject of great interest to us both and it helps us to practice awareness.

We are fortunate that we can meet for lunch every day. It's our soul mate love date! The deep discussions we have are almost unimaginable the way they feed our souls and boost each other!

It sometimes creates tremendous synchronicities, when we discover we have both been contemplating the same things - joining a gym, reading a book on a same or similar subject, going to a conference, handling a situation, changing an attitude, creating a practice from using a new spiritual skill, or even thinking of a trip.

For our entire marriage, we have taken Fridays off work to be together. It's our soul day. It's amazingly helpful to dedicate some day or time that is set aside and treasured as soul mate love time. In fact, it's imperative. We also have problem-solving discussions as well. Money is a big topic. We start from the premise that our consciousness is the generator of our income and job and career opportunities. We think of ourselves as love trillionares. It's funny, but true. That puts "wealth" into soul perspective.

Although Scotty has had a successful real estate career, still, when there's been a recession and our income has been cut by a large percent, we have had to borrow money from our home equity line, hoping we can repay it as soon as possible, which we usually do.

However, it's hard to get ahead unless we have a steadiness of good years. Still, we always address any material, human condition as souls or Higher Self.

We remind ourselves that our souls brought everything with us into the human experience that we need for this life. And we remember that we have divine power to manifest all that's needed. It's worked well for us for 25 years, providing for our human needs.

Everything and everyone receives prayer in our household. As souls, we bring spiritual elevation to our earthly weights and burdens. We shed light on dark areas of thought. And we boldly go where no one has been, addressing hardships through our metaphysics and earnest, ongoing prayers (mostly listening to divine guidance which pours in).

Our first and final prayer is always to listen for divine guidance which we receive through intuition. As a result, our lives have been loaded with lovely surprises of outcomes that we ourselves could not have produced without divine help. We all need this! How on earth could anyone get through the daunting human experience without prayer and facing all obstacles as your Higher Self or soul – allowing yourself to be guided.

As best friends, we want to be together endlessly. Even though we each have independence from each other during most of the day, (except lunches) our unions are dynamic, meaningful, and loaded with love and fun! Most of our interests overlap and feed each other continually.

Recently, at a special lunch, Shannon had typed out metaphysical treatments for Scotty regarding a couple of his physical concerns. Healing commenced. We felt closer than ever through this joint effort to combine our prayers, elevate our thoughts, and allow more light to enter our consciousness, which would lead to healing. We do this for each other regularly.

Sometimes a person's lovely qualities are so visible that they are loud and clear. The closer someone is living to their Higher Self, the more evident are their beautiful qualities. But someone doesn't have to be the Dahlia Lama in order to have their Higher Self recognized by you.

With most people, you may need to look for it. But as you become observant, over time, a person's spiritual qualities become apparent. Just because this may be a new practice for you shouldn't prevent you from making strong efforts to put these new skills into action. What are your waiting for? You are the one who will have to initiate this. The better you get at this, the more soul will be revealed. Hello soul!

Often, when we discover someone is engaged and getting married, we ask them, "What is it that you most love about him or her?" The answer is usually very simple. Usually with the mix of adjectives, we'll hear how kind or patient the person is and how much they love being together. To us, this qualifies as gigantic and will most likely lead to lasting love.

The power of kindness

Do you know how hard it is to be characterized as kind?

It's one of the hardest things to maintain in a relationship. Involved in kindness is a lot of deep motivation to express patience, respect, empathy, peacemaking, and caring to others.

There's tremendous empathy & gentleness in kindness. It requires a great deal of discipline.

Love thrives in such fertile environments for the heart. Kindness points to an evolved soul. When you're looking for a soul mate, look for kindness! In Sanskrit, one of the most revered words to describe living a spiritual path is ahimsa. It means consideration. And the opposite word, himsa, means harmful, not considerate. Which one do you think is more spiritual? Which one do you think most keeps the heart open and ready to love? Which one connotes kindness?

We are tender, fragile beings.

When our heart feels wounded by unkind words or actions, we shut down. Some people encounter so much himsa that they no longer open their hearts. But this is where we can most grow as well.

Forgiveness is essential to soul mate relationships where each will surely make mistakes

We are here to grow. Unless we can forgive and move forward from our stories and events of being hurt, we can't engage in things of the heart. We become closed off, protective, and perhaps angry. When we do, we cut off love. Is that really what you want?

And it's the same with others who you wish to be in a relationship with. If they can't forgive you when you make a mistake and when you offer your sincere apology from the heart, they won't be able to participate in a loving relationship with you. It's better to accept it and move on. Their being in a stuck position and unwilling to make an effort to grow doesn't mean you are also stuck.

Love and commitment come with soul responsibilities

Being the person who is closest to your soul mate means that you will each be the most likely person to be called in a crisis. These are opportunities for really growing your soul mate love.

Loving someone comes with responsibilities of looking after each other. Having each other's back means there needs to be reliability and accountability. It's part of grown-up love.

This is an area where you can each shine, even before the crises.

For example, if your loved one isn't feeling well, there's a loving response that greatly adds to the relationship. Don't wait until they're in the bed with fever! Illnesses often have an onset period. Sometimes illness can be offset by being mindful and taking early steps to avoid it. Notice when your love mate has lower energy or is a little "off."

See how you can be helpful, asking your beloved to share how they are feeling, not only with symptoms but also emotions as well. Illness often has an emotional component.

Your loved one will feel loved and cared for by these nurturing check in's. Never miss an opportunity to do this. It connects in a way that nothing else does.

Asking if they want you to bring water, help them to bed, needing a blanket or pillow, make dinner, make a doctor appointment, or being encouraged to rest or take supplements are all part of what a mature loving relationship looks like. It deepens the soul connection. Love cares. And it shows its caring in many ways, whether or not it's convenient.

Rather than making excuses, love eagerly steps in to offer help & comfort. Isn't this what you'd like to receive if you needed to feel better? This is a kind thing to offer.

Things you can do to come closer

What percent of the time are you tired, stressed, or struggling with an issue?

These are times that love shows up.

Show daily interest in your loved one's welfare. Ask about their day. Listen and respond. If it was a hard day, find words to convey you care.

Put yourself in their shoes. What attitudes could someone show you that would bring you comfort and cushion your day?

Here are a few easy questions you can ask:

- I'm sorry you've had a hard day. Would you like to sit down and tell me about it? How about a cup of tea while we chat?
- What would you most like to share with me?
- What does your soul want me to know right now?
- What do you most need?
- What can I can do to help?

Just listen, offering your kind attention and understanding. Sometimes that's all we need to feel better.

If you have an idea that may offer them some relief, ask if you can share it. But otherwise, don't try to rush in and fix the problems of their day. Just listening can be so very helpful where they themselves can see through the problem and let the light in.

During hard times, we pray for each other. Actually, we pray for each other each day regardless. And we often share our prayers afterwards, revealing in what way our loved one was on our mind and how deeply we wish them blessings in every area.

Hearing that your loved is praying and asking for divine support in your behalf has a very healing effect and touches the heart.

Resonance

A big way to get closer to your soul mate is through resonance.

Here are a couple examples.

We had a crystal singing bowl that played F#, the frequency of the high heart chakra. Every time we rang it, the sound immediately vibrated within our hearts, opening us to the universe and beyond. And we felt at one with everyone, everywhere. It was totally blissful.

One day the crystal bowl broke into a hundred pieces. At first, we were so disappointed. But, as our lives evolved, we realized that the love resonance of the bowl was still with us.

What can you do to feel more resonance?

Notice when your Higher Self comes into resonance with someone. Often, it comes as a result of feeling a heart swell of immense gratitude or joy, and it's felt especially when you use your voice to speak a personal acknowledgment for who they are and what it means to know them.

This is the language of soul mates. It spills over to others. You recognize it connecting with them as you spill. It's incredibly intimate.

It's one level of love when we feel it. It's another, additional level of love when we speak it. Most people don't speak even a fraction of their love. Big mistake. Voiced love is powerful!

Whenever we feel emotionally safe, our hearts start to open. There are times in our personal relationship where we feel so much love that it's as though we become love itself. Bliss has a way of knowing no limits. It's so interconnected that you hardly know where one self ends or the other begins. The rare feeling of oneness is transforming.

The feeling of love creates chemicals in the brain which are elated. All of this causes us to have a very high love permeation factor. It becomes its own presence, connecting with our soul mate and feeling endlessly connected to all. It creates a feeling of overall wellness within and to others around us. This is a powerful energy field.

You may also feel this deep connection when making love where there is great tenderness, respect, and empathy expressed regarding each other and felt within your touch and movements.

Another way of coming closer to your love is through permeation, just as a fragrance can have a permeation factor.

Think of a lovely fragrance, such as lavender, when it permeates the atmosphere. We are instantly lifted, soothed, and calmed. A sense of well-being comes over us.

Let the love you are feeling (whether it's from gratitude, joy, or feeling loved yourself) move out from you and expand, penetrating your love mate with this powerful force of connectedness, lifting them to new heights, bringing them into a place of joy, and discovering their world now permeating with love.

When you come into resonance or have the experience of permeation, there's an other-world feeling about it that transports you ethereally. It's a different dimension and way of experiencing extraordinary closeness.

When we're together, we are aware of each other's resonance, even when we're not talking. It feels like a presence that carries a familiar and loving quality, one that brings great comfort and refuge.

We never actually make an effort to create these close experiences. They occur naturally when the conditions are right. As you become aware of them, they will start to happen. When they do, be sure to show your appreciation. Take nothing for granted. Every effort you are making is having a positive impact on them as well as you.

These are some of the ways that love blesses us. Infuse your environment with love by practicing the awareness of what's possible. Be ready to honor. Look for ways. Stay open to the possibilities of your soul's greatest gifts.

Chapter 9

Soul Tension
How Soul Mates Resolve Conflict

It requires refined love skills to learn how to address a conflict with your soul mate.

The goal in soul mate love is to handle the conflict without hurting or harming your soul mate, while speaking in a respectful and considerate way yet simultaneously forging through to make your point in a loving way. And listening.

When there's conflict

It helps to keep in mind during conflicts, that you are both on the same side and you both can hardly wait to work through the conflict to get back to your rainbow connection of love.

However, how you handle a conflict could actually harm the love connection, depending on whether or not you hurt your soul mate's feelings or your soul mate feels insulted or criticized.

Our faults are not really personal. We are all learning and growing from the ego's hardships and blindness which keep showing up in our relationships. To a certain degree, we each come with our baggage. Then, hopefully, as you evolve, you begin to see "my story" as a big, fat imposition to everything you want in soul mate love. It's in the way! And it's a wakeup call from your soul!

When you learn and grow in ways of working through conflict with your soul mate, you will find ways of loving that you never imagined just because you want this to go well, without division.

The result may feel so beautiful that it feels almost magical, as love often does. But there's nothing magical about the love skills set into motion during a conflict. It breeds maturity into the heart.

And, with each effort, your determination to keep harmony during conflict will weave an invisible grid of love throughout the universe. Your soul mate will see your efforts and your hearts will stay connected. Your soul mate will feel appreciated for the extraordinary devotion you are making to maintain the quality of your soul mate love. This is true love!

Disagreements or clashes can occur

During times of clashes, each one needs to be mindful of their speech, to keep it respectful.

Nothing erodes a relationship more than anger, harsh words, judgments, criticisms, raised voices, and exasperated facial expressions.

When you need to speak up, choose your words carefully and lay no blame or judgments that fall hard on the heart. Take your time and go slowly. Let love guide your feelings and words.

Whoever has the frustration or hurt has to be careful about explaining it because it will surely make your loved one feel defensive. And when that occurs, you may not even be able to explain your problem because of the interruptions or a defensive wall. And that will add to your frustration and anger.

Sometimes our greatest offering is to listen. Great souls know the power of this act of love where you are alert not to interrupt or to judge, but to give your full attention and freedom so that your soul mate can get in touch with their feelings and hear themselves think, which, alone, may arrive at the solution.

Powerful shifts can occur through loving attention given each other, through the great skill of active listening.

The one who is most upset can go first. It's important to be allowed to gently speak through their frustrations and problem, as they see it, so it can be fully understood.

In listening and keeping the space quiet, you are showing great respect at a very sensitive time to your loved one. It helps! They will feel your love.

That's always the point in a loving relationship, to feel the love.

You may be working overtime in your heart to hold back your own side of the story, but your restraint will have enormous love rewards.

Once they are finished, you can ask, "Are you complete? Is there anything else?" If not, you can have a turn, first sharing your concern, then reflecting back what you think you heard them say and how it must feel to them. When you are finished, ask if you got it about right. And if there is anything else they would like to add.

Often, after one of us has talked, the other one will say, "Tell me more." And another entire avalanche of feelings will roll out. And, as it does, it also gets cleared. This is the power of listening.

These techniques are life savers. They bring enormous gratitude and act as one of our great gifts of love to the soul.

The Healing Force of Love

by Scottyg

Hello anger
you seem about to burst

I will sit with you until the pain subsides

Do you ever imagine
your life with no anger at all?

Love has asked me to send this message
for you to store
in the inbox of your heart

I'm so sorry for your suffering
but know this sweet friend

No anger within you
can withstand the healing force
of my love

And I will never stop

loving

You!

123

Harmony in your relationship is a way of showing your love

We don't argue.

When we disagree on a decision, we wait for a choice that we <u>both</u> agree on – whether it's a choice of how to budget our money, what to do about a family member, where to go out, or anything else.

Each of us would rather give up our first choice and wait for a better solution, in order to enjoy something we'll both like, because harmony is so important to us. It's our first rule.

The soul thrives on harmony.

When there's discord, hurt feelings, disagreements, misunderstandings, or miscommunications, the soul stagnates until there's a clearing.

Can you imagine anything so important than to clear the way for your souls to shine and love once again? Treat it as a process that needs to occur in order to clear discord. It doesn't have to take a long time either.

On those times when we get stuck, it's important to take time out to reflect on what has happened and to calm ourselves.

A few moments of sitting quietly while focusing on following the breath, offers space to begin seeing past emotions and into what's at the bottom of the problem. It helps to create mindfulness about the words you will choose to address the situation as well as what you want the outcome to be - hearts again close, eyes smiling. Calming is an important part of the process of healing discord.

Often, one of us will extend an apology in case we created a problem for the other.

An apology doesn't mean you actually did something wrong or that you assume responsibility. An apology, rather than blaming, keeps hearts soft.

An apology is a peace offering showing you didn't mean any harm, that the error was not intended, and that you want to come back into sync with your wonderful souls.

An apology also offers an opportunity if you yourself were caught off guard, from a resentment surfacing within you. It happens.

We are protective to each other's happiness. We want the other to be happy, to have good feelings about themselves and their life, as well as to feel good about us as their soul mate. Our hearts want to endlessly bless the other with everything good.

The idea is to enjoy each other and our lives as much as possible and during tough periods, sustain our joy with spiritual practices, a positive outlook, mindfulness, and great love as we work through these areas, trying to learn whatever we can and grow in character and heart love.

When trouble hits and you become angry, or when you find yourself overwhelmed by a difficult situation, then, of course, it affects your mood and outlook.

And if the trouble lasts for days or weeks or longer, it will also affect sleep patterns which add to the mix of difficulty. If it persists, the troublesome problem adds negative emotions, making it seem very personal, even questioning yourself.

When one of us is triggered, we are each careful and protective not to take it out on the other. We talk it over (a lot), pray, and we offer each other full support with empathy and compassion to the point we really feel it accompanying us when we are apart.

Our hearts become more tender, knowing how hard it is to move through these situations. Keep noticing: this loving response to difficult times is what soul mate love looks like!

Negative emotions need to be cleared. This is what goes on in a normal life. You can't ignore your feelings. If you try to stuff them down, they'll rise up and create a potential, out-of-control explosion, which you'll deeply regret.

Mature, loving people understand this. Just take your time. Sleep on it. Try to maintain patience and your equilibrium.

Good will is important. We help each other through these periods as much as possible. We talk about our feelings, try to come into acceptance with the way things are while also seeing if there's something we can do about the situation to make it better, and we keep our attitude in check as much as possible.

Self-control is not only admirable, it's also important for maintaining mutual harmony with your soul mate.

Remaining civil and keeping the peace is a way of showing your love. It takes patience and sometimes, great restraint. And it generally requires spiritual practices as well, such as:

- Prayer.
- Sitting quietly, reflecting.
- Asking for divine guidance.
- Letting go.
- Seeing it from a soul perspective of Higher Selves.
- Offering your kind understanding.

We have a treasure chest full of these spiritual skills and we use them regularly.

Problems need resolution.

They are opportunities for growth, which is the path of the soul.

This is the important work of a soul to move through human predicaments with grace using skills for learning.

If you are a soul mate, you understand what is at stake. You don't retreat.

We hope to address human problems as a soul, as one who has incarnated to love and to bring our gifts of help to others.

We are also aware that we are here to deepen our awareness and to learn and grow.

We are full of hope that we can lessen our and other's pain while we do this. And not to add to another's pain. It's a tricky road.

And it's impossible to do it without a lot of mistakes. We do best if we're supported and loved by a soul mate while we try to achieve this awesome task.

We heard Eckhart Tolle say, "Accept the moment as if you had chosen it." And in answer to "How do I know that this is the experience that I need?" He answered, "Because this is what you are experiencing."

The soul is on a journey of awakening. The universal healer is love.

No matter how difficult life gets, soul mates offer their love which can do wonders to help advance each other's journey of love and awakening.

There is nothing happier than two souls doing this together - learning, growing, and gaining wisdom, while being loved to their bones.

Souls also delight in self-expression. An awakened soul learns myriad ways to express the divine Self while in the human experience.

Releasing and letting go of old ways we've outgrown is sometimes a difficult road. Love softens the load and brightens the way.

We know whenever the other is struggling. And we make strong and immediate efforts to step forward with big empathy and a sincere offer to help in any way.

No one is perfect. And certainly, we are not.

Keep giving your love in ways that celebrate and help the other. Show your appreciation and speak it. Tell your mate what you most love about him or her. Make a list. Do this often and keep adding to the list with honesty.

Neither of us take on the responsibility to fix the other when down. Our love is more in the category of support spoken, interest and caring shown, and check in's. We never ignore a problem.

When you offer to take time to listen, this is a huge offering. It's worth a discussion on agreeing on a best time to do this and deciding where is a good, quiet place where you won't be interrupted.

Your swiftness in offering your help on the same day of the upset will quadruple the evidence of your love. It's needed.

Sometimes we get overwhelmed and can't see our way through the maze. This is where soul mates shine because this is the work of each soul. And when we do it as soul work, we are tremendous in moving past these mine fields.

Since no one knows your soul mate as you do, you are also significant in spotting when they are suffering and don't even know it because they are embroiled in it.

As humans, we are often distracted and become bombarded. By bringing this to your soul mate's attention, that you know they are suffering even though they haven't expressed it, you can potentially alleviate further suffering by helping them to address it.

Sometimes, just trying to keep up with daunting changes in our lives, as well as coping with ongoing stresses and pressures, keeping up with paying the bills, and doing a good job at work, or getting along with a difficult boss, or other conflicts that arise in our lives can really undo us. Some times are harder than others.

We are most valuable and appreciated when we are being understanding, tender, caring, helpful, and reminding our soul mate of their fantastic traits.

You will soon see how quickly they have forgotten and need to be reminded that they are wonderful, good, and an important soul on a mission that is truly making a difference to themselves and others. This is what soul mate love does!

We aspire to live in the present and practice awareness. We live fairly close to these spiritual practices so it doesn't take much for us to come back to center or at least to be aware that there's something which needs to be addressed by one of us. We often share which skills we are using and how it is most helpful.

The practice of awareness often pulls us back home as we become aware of our needs and the needs of the other, in order to take stock of the situation.

As soul mates, we focus on the path before us. It is powerful, during hard times, to remember that what we are facing is more than just a bad mood, the loss of a job, grieving over the loss of a loved one, stress, frustration, or losing faith in ourselves or another.

No matter what the problem is disguised as, the most important thing you need to remember is that this is an opportunity your soul signed up for in order to awaken. And it's important. This is your work as a soul.

Any time you can remind your soul mate of this, is a good time. As souls, we intend to put heart and soul into our earth time in order to rise higher to the light of love and have everyone rise with us.

We can each do our part in this. Everyone is affected by each soul. The work is serious and often painstaking. We will make a million mistakes where we'll have to learn to forgive ourselves over and over. And to forgive each other over and over.

The goal is divine. We are making every effort to bring our divinity into the human experience. Not an easy task.

We need to be soul oriented in order to achieve what we came to do. Most of the world is not oriented towards the soul. Those who are will have to be the ones who remember. And as they remember to come back to their divine Selves, they will be holding the light up for all others.

Earlier in our lives, we were not as awake to soul as we are today. But during those earlier times, other souls, who were awake, were doing their work, affecting us in our own awakening so that today we are more fully awake. That's how it works. We are all here to help the awakening. This is how soul mates think. This is our approach.

We try to drop our story of rehearsing being wronged and come back to our light where we are then available to shine within ourselves and then outward, to others.

It really helps to clear things and not hold them in. Anger, disappointments, and frustrations pile up and need a healthy release valve. Talking it over (as peacefully as possible) can be healing.

During times when you can be fully open to the moment, you can live in the spaciousness of unlimited possibilities for yourself and your soul mate, as well as for every sentient being on earth and beyond. These are wonderful opportunities for the soul!

One of our greatest challenges in the human experience, one which distracts us from our soul work and robs us of living as awakened souls, is fear.

It creeps in everywhere. Fear of not having enough money, love, health, time, opportunities, recognition, respect, – you name it! Fear creates opposition, fighting, and war. It murders. And it's straight from the ego, the false sense of self.

What does a soul, the divine Self, do with this highly charged negative emotion?

First of all, take a few deep breaths as you allow yourself to become calm.

Then, move towards observing the fear. Observation places a tiny space between you and the fear. It changes the status of fear from "my" fear to "the" fear. This is the process of awakening.

These tools you use for yourself will be welcomed as powerful support to your soul mate when trouble of any kind comes in. These are moments which are loaded with great opportunities for the soul.

Let's face it. Anyone can cave in to fear, be grouchy, blame others, argue and degrade, or make excuses for why they are always the victim or why they always lose out.

At what point does your soul begin to engage in its vitally life-changing work? It's at those very moments which are most crucial to your soul's work.

How many red flags does a soul need to see before they begin a practice to rise and make every effort to live from their light rather than from the illusion that they are not of the light?

It's hard on your soul mate when you refuse to rouse yourself or stay stuck in old patterns of hating yourself.

And it prevents soul mate love from flowing into those really high vibrational patterns that we are capable of – patterns which keep us inspired, awestruck, and engaged in miracles unfolding before us. Patterns where synchronicities appear out of nowhere providing exactly what we most need.

The benefits of making every effort to live out from your soul self, especially as a soul mate, are endless and extraordinary and open your heart and mind to bliss states. How happy is that!

Learning from the trees

Tree scientists have learned an important lesson about how vibrational input matters profoundly.

By studying communications between trees, even among their roots, scientists have seen evidence that trees are capable of alerting each other and boosting each other's immune systems when vulnerable.

Imagine the trees of our world having these ongoing connections! Such love and purpose!

Think of this whenever you wonder if your generous efforts are making any difference.

As souls, we are engaged in natural communications to bless each other. We're made to do this.

We are engaged in a network of love that is inescapable! This is the purpose of our souls.

Awakened souls are aware of what is at stake. A soul mate's ongoing love can lend tremendous support to each other's growth, ease, comfort, openings of possibilities, spiritual power, and life happiness.

We need each other to cope with change, insecurities, and uncertainties. Love is bigger than all the combined problems in the entire human experience. When put to the test, love can overwhelm our problems.

Being on a love team is like nothing else. Keeping love alive, we talk about it, show enormous appreciation, lavish with compliments, and praise.

We are generous hearted, never withholding our love for any reason, just as we hope our mate offers us the same loving treatment.

In this powerful soul energy, tension dissolves. This is the path of soul mate love.

Chapter 10

Quantum Soul Leaps

When soul mate love grows, the ability to explore and identify each other's soul expands exponentially.

There is a great desire to know, at a deeper level, "Who am I?" and "What is my soul's purpose?"

There is a tremendous joy in helping each other answer these questions. It is often easier for one soul mate to see into the soul's purpose of the other than that person can see him or herself.

Over the years, we have shared invaluable insights on each other's souls.

It started when we were dating. We used words to describe what we were learning about each other's essence. And for many years, these words expanded and found their way regularly into our conversations being hailed as each other's greatest value.

As our love grew and also our spirituality and state of awakening grew, so did our ability to share insights on each other.

What happens in spiritual growth, as it evolves over a period of time, is that it takes on a shape. This is what happened as a result of sharing our essence over the years, when_Shannon received an even clearer image of Scott. It came from deep intuition. She shared her view of his Higher Self in the following way.

She described him as a yellow grid that stretched the expansion of the universe, underlying all that is and influencing everything and everywhere.

Using colored pencils, she drew planet earth and stars and beyond. And throughout the picture, she overlaid a yellow net, indicating Scotty's beautiful soul. It felt very real to us both. And it was the first time that she had gained an image to describe his soul.

She began calling him the Yellow Grid. One of the big characteristics of the Yellow Grid is being a unifier. This insight was invaluable to Scott

Being in real estate calls for massive unifying skills. This is an area where Scott shines.

Over and over and over, in times of crises where a home sale looked as though it was going to collapse, or where negotiations would break down between parties, or where there was contention coming from the client, Scotty developed an overdrive combining qualities of calmness and non-forcefulness, along with deep listening, in order to hold things together.

His gentle kindness and patience were as powerful as the Colorado River carving out the Grand Canyon.

He kept an ongoing open conversation as the differences slowly moved towards peaceful solutions. It worked. Over time, these responses to crises revealed and shaped his peace-making skills and deepened his spirituality, revealing to us both how powerful unity is. And how deeply unity runs within him. It's really important to him.

Can you imagine how, by identifying these skills within Scott, they grew? And how much this added to his joy and confidence? We were discovering an important and beautiful aspect of his Higher Self.

The same has occurred with Shannon.

At this same time of identifying Scott as the Yellow Grid, she had an image of herself as Mother Love, covering earth, and enveloping it in comfort and healing. Her color was deep blue with some aqua. This view felt deeply accurate.

Now we had, for the first time, images of each other's soul. This was an evolutionary shift for us.

It's no surprise Shannon had been identified with healing love. It's who she is. In her many years of spiritual healing with clients, they not only experienced healing, but the depth of Mother Love. Not surprisingly, many clients referred to her as Mother.

Within this identity, she was also a longtime caretaker to her parents and an incredible love support to her daughter & grandson. She brooded over loved ones in their hard times and enveloped them with her love. She prayed and offered healing insights, holding them dear to her heart.

You could feel the love coming from her heart as she nurtured and comforted through her caring words, over and over and over with her Mother Love. And her spiritual power grew!

These identifications are markers where we find ourselves within each other's hearts. Over time, by identifying each other, we strengthen who we are and rise even higher through the clarity and confidence it inspires. We talk about this a lot. It's one of our favorite subjects!

These spiritual images became a short cut in our conversations where we could quickly remind each other how we were being viewed and to be called back.

We came to realize that what we were viewing about each other was our Higher Selves. It's a rare and special insight which grows from deep acknowledgment.

The Higher Self is the divine self. It's the self usually hidden from the world because it's quiet, invisible, and mostly left unacknowledged. And yet, it's the finest aspect of each one of us. It's the final proof that God is, indeed, present, acting through each one of us, as a soul.

It's a God sign.

Who doesn't need that! And to have that alive within our relationship is a living presence of the divine, reminding us that we are of a divine nature and origin. In fact, all of us are!

It's our favorite thing, to continue looking at each other's Higher Self, and acknowledge how we see it. This is the hallmark of our soul mate love. It causes our souls to soar. And it nurtures our feelings of being loved to our bones!

This has caused our intuitive senses to expand far beyond what we ever imagined, offering insights into our divine identities. It's where we live in the laboratory of watching for more to be revealed. And more comes.

This practice of looking into the divine depths of each other, has tremendously expanded our consciousness, leading us to places we never dreamed.

One of the main outcomes of this has been to rise in our spiritual power. Can you imagine praying from your Higher Self? This is especially powerful when we, as souls, offer healing.

Past life soul regressions - a quantum soul leap

Past life regressions have hit mainstream. In psychological practices, they are used as a powerful aid to address and clear post-traumatic stress disorder as well as to bring forth self-awakenings.

In spiritual practices, past life "soul" regressions are used to reveal more of the person's soul.

141

When Shannon first read about past life soul regressions, what appealed to her was less about a past life and more about where we go in between lives. What's that all about? What happens to us when we exist as pure spiritual consciousness, in between incarnations?

Here's a big soul mate love secret. Scotty here.

When your soul partner gets passionate about something new, pay attention, and listen deeply.

We were on vacation and Shannon was reading a book by Dr. Linda Backman called "The Evolving Soul: Spiritual Healing through Past Life Exploration."

She said to me, "I'd like to get trained in giving past life regressions, but I need a girlfriend to do it with because I want to receive this opportunity too, not just give it to others."

At that moment, I realized that I might have to be that girlfriend, even though my interest level was lower than Shannon's.

During the following months, we were both trained to give "past life soul regressions" by Dr. Backman, and then trained again by her to give "between lives soul regressions." The latter was what interested Shannon the most.

And what a soul surprise it turned out to be for me.

During my entire life, the two biggest leaps upwards in life for me were, one, meeting Shannon, and two, how my identity shifted so much higher through between lives soul regressions.

We've given each other more than 40 soul regressions! Shannon's dream came true!

Spirit World

In "between lives soul regressions," this is where pure soul is revealed.

We call it Spirit World.

With facilitation from the regressionist, the entire session is guided by your spiritual guides and teachers.

When Shannon decided to experience a soul regression, it was life changing and offered her immense insights identifying her own soul. What transpired, when she made an appointment with a professional regressionist, was almost unbelievable to her.

Slowing the brain wave down through relaxation techniques, she entered Theta brain wave, a very slow brain wave that occurs just before sleep. In this brain wave, there is immense lucidity and vast spiritual insight.

If we try and explain our out-of-this-world experience, it might not mean much to you. But we want to expose you to it, because it reveals how much more there is to each one of us. And it reveals the vastness of our divine selves. This enables us to bring our soul's spiritual power to offer healing to the world.

We want this for your soul too!

We know that your soul leaps will look completely unique in the world of infinite possibilities, but we are sharing what has happened to us in the spirit of opening you to higher possibilities of soul expansion.

Here goes.

Shannon's Quantum Leap

During her "between life soul regression," Shannon was shown an image of a cosmically large and enormously loving figure. It was a woman made of light and color. Her presence was one of total love.

Shannon burst into tears at the sight of her. Her robe of white light trailed 27,000 miles long. Within her heart area were intense colors of illuminated deep blue and golden yellow. Her name was Mary. Her powerful band of angels always accompany her.

During this regression, Shannon was asked to look in the mirror and share what she saw. She looked in the mirror and was astonished that she saw Mary! Shannon's guides were revealing to her that she was the very same image of light and love that she had just viewed!

Over the course of many more soul regressions, this was a repeating theme. And over many regressions, Shannon visited the healing explosive region of Mary's crown chakra, as well as her heart chakra of pure love.

It was revealed that Mary was Mother of Love. She is a universal symbol of love and healing. This seemed to build on Shannon's earlier insight when she saw herself as Mother Love who nurtured earth.

Many of our souls represent Mary. Perhaps yours does too. Our souls each take on magnificent roles when we incarnate! You cannot even imagine the beauty and magnificence of your own soul!

In other soul regressions, Shannon has experienced the moment she was created and shot forth directly from Source. And in other times, she has found herself in a state of pure awareness, before time and activity, before the world was. And it was revealed to her how life and breath came into being at its onset.

Many regressions showed Shannon in a past life standing in contemplation and awareness, overlooking the sea.

Her past lives were less about events and people and more about her state of being - in stillness and awareness and contemplation. She has come to realize that this is what she does best today in her human experience when she connects deeply with her soul.

Here's her drawing describing the way her soul evolves and grows.

Through between lives soul regressions, Shannon began to learn how she is an Origin being, one who dwells at Source. It characterizes her human life as well.

For example, when someone needs healing, she is guided by insights that come from a divine, original source. Shannon channels Source. Her regressions have increased her ability to do this. Maybe it's because her confidence has grown.

For decades, she identified herself as a spiritual healer. Now she sees that, through healing insights, she unites a person with Source. It's done through the power of divine Love. And it's very healing.

During one of Shannon's regressions, she felt an awareness of the healing energy that accompanied Jesus. And as each of Jesus' healings took place, she was a healing energy within it – the lame man, the blind, the woman with issues of blood and on and on. Shannon was right there. She was a conscious energy of pure love. That's what her soul was doing at that time.

Perhaps your soul was doing the same.

See how many vast aspects there are to a soul? And it feels as though Shannon has just begun to pull back the curtain on these epic discoveries.

These out-of-this-world experiences have been poignant and have integrated themselves as reminders of Shannon's immortal soul. It's who she is.

Now, she pulls in these reminders in her daily life, which helps her to identify herself and live more as a spiritual being having a human experience. It makes all the difference to live this way.

Each of our souls is equally this magnificent.

We tend to deny it and create disclaimers throwing up road blocks by judging ourselves as egomaniacs or selfish. We wiggle and squirm to think of ourselves in our spiritual greatness, but it's there within each one of us.

It's within you two!

Scott's Quantum Leap

Scott's evolution has revealed even more than the sense of being a yellow grid.

In one of his soul regressions, he met the Golden Light. Often, when we have these startling insights, spontaneous tears emerge from the exquisite beauty we are beholding. We can hardly believe what we are being shown!

It was no less with Scott. During a series of many soul regressions, it was shown to him that he is a Golden Light. Its presence is beautiful with bright love that encompasses everything, everywhere.

He saw millions of others as Golden Light beings too.

One soul characteristic of Golden Light is everywhereness. As Golden Light, he can be at one place and then simultaneously at another place. He has a presence that goes everywhere – and every*when* - at once. Golden Light encompasses allness.

Doesn't this sound like a yellow grid that Shannon had perceived decades earlier?

Shannon often experiences the "everywhere and everywhen" aspects of his soul as a presence which permeates. It has a calming, healing effect.

What's your soul name?

What if you could rename yourself with a name that identified your soul. What would that be?

A long time ago, Scott taught English-as-a-second-language to adults of multiple nationalities. The Hispanic students nicknamed him "Scotty" with a warmth and tenderness that reached Scott's heart. He began to think of himself as Scotty – and that's what his friends call him today.

After Scott's initiation into the Golden Light, he stepped further into soul and began writing a few soul poems under the name of "Scottyg" – the "g" standing for Golden Light.

Even though no one knew Scotty by this name, it felt good to him to explore identifying himself as a soul being. Some of his poems are sprinkled throughout this book.

These "soul names" aren't public nicknames. They are simply present in the privateness of our lives together and, unless we were writing this book on the inside secrets in our soul mate love, no one would know. It's just one more way we stay tuned in to soul together.

Often, we call each other by our soul names, Golden Light and Mary. It helps to keep us awake to who we are.

So, if you were joining us in this spiritual nickname soul adventure, what would your soul name be?

It has been Scotty's long practice, to take quiet reflection time before he goes to bed. During that time, he writes down names of people or groups and what suffering they may be experiencing.

Then he writes to the side of each name, or situation, a spiritual insight that brings healing to each problem. It's both healing and empowering. Shannon loves waking up to breakfast where he shares his insights from the previous evening. And Shannon often has pages of insights as well that she shares.

Scotty has saved some of the pages over the years. In fact, we both have had tons of pages everywhere with spiritual insights that felt too important to throw away! Then, from time to time we have trashed them and started over with fresh inspiration.

Now, since his iPad pro, where he can doodle, these evening devotions have often evolved with images.

Here's one of these simple spiritual drawings. It represents how he sees Shannon as a holy woman of light, radiating light and healing – including many healing "away missions." Needless to say, we're Star Trek fans.

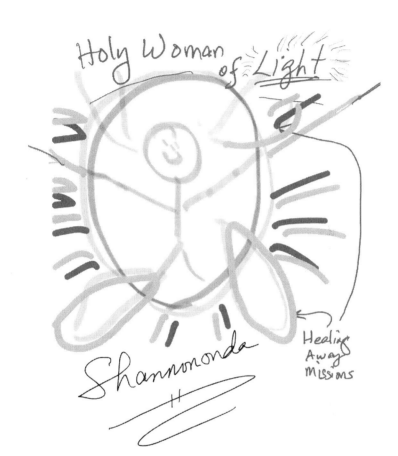

See how things evolve in exploring soul?

And, this has also happened with Shannon.

On Scott's last birthday, Shannon gave him further insights on his soul. When she prayerfully opened to seeing more of his soul, the term "Indra's Net" came to her mind.

As she researched Indra's Net, it helped her to expand the description of how she saw Scott's soul.

The net is a mythological theory from about 2500 years ago.

The myth reveals a universal jeweled net, exquisitely connecting everything as one. It represents total unity. And it has the ability to permeate everything, everywhere.

Joseph Campbell refers to Indra's Net as universal connectedness, the opposite of the illusion of separateness. It's as though there were a unifying, single principle behind all creation.

At Scotty's birthday lunch, she presented him with images and full descriptions of Indra's Net and how she saw that it described Scotty's true divine Self. He prominently carries this within his soul.

It created a magical birthday of great soulful awakening. She brought pages and pictures to their birthday lunch, which brought forth a two-hour soulful discussion that thrilled us both.

Here's one of the pictures of Indra's Net that she printed out for him on his birthday. We are explorers of soul! See how quantum?

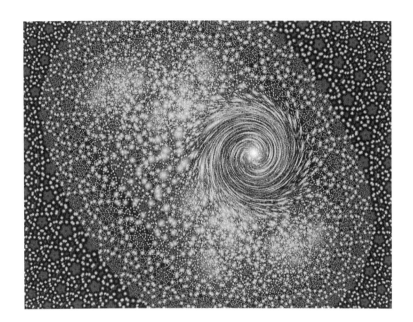

Universal Soul Healing

One thing we love doing together – a soul calling really – is to address the news of current world events, the state of nations and leaders, disasters, refugees, violence, injustices, the environment, and the poor, as well as the direction which our earthly souls are heading.

This is where we direct our greatest power for healing. The work is immensely important to each of us.

We find that the more awakened we are as souls (identifying and expanding our understanding of what it means to be spiritual), the more power packed our healing treatments are. This is wonderful news to our souls, which deeply want to help make a better world.

We all share life on earth together as a vital soul pod.

Doing this work as two souls who come together to share the world's load, is an extension of our shared love. It is deeply meaningful to us to address world problems together. This is a quantum soul leap into living big. This is high on our list of important values to practice. Our souls are devoted to healing.

We often use our soul images, Golden Light or Mary, as images of truth, to counter problems. Since they represent the true self and the true reality, every problem can be considered an illusion.

You may find that to be a stretch, but this is radical healing from the soul. It is very effective and it represents quantum soul leaps.

The Fibonacci opening in your love life

Scott had an amazing between lives soul regression just as we were finishing this book. He saw that we are all on a path of Light, whether we even know it or not. He recounted how many "very difficult" events have reshaped our lives. In each case, what seemed like a terrible loss opened us to more light.

Looking back, the losses promoted our growth in light. In each occurrence of darkness, we moved to a much better place – and we moved there exponentially.

At the time of the loss, however, the darkness seemed overwhelmingly negative. For example, each of us suffered through many years of an unhappy marriage. There seemed to be no exit. When the exit did come, it seemed like a great loss.

But here we are, today, writing this book on soul mate love from a state of love bliss we've now enjoyed for 25 years.

That's a shift in light that was – and is - exponential. We didn't just incrementally improve from bad marriages to a better marriage. We leaped exponentially into a new level of love we hadn't even imagined.

That's the natural path of exponential light. And you are on this path!

At a Star Knowledge conference recently, we were introduced to the Fibonacci number sequence of exponential expansion, named after Fibonacci, an Italian mathematician who lived about 750 years ago.

In the Fibonacci sequence, as the diagram shows, the numbers multiply exponentially. This pattern of expansion is present throughout nature. An example is the spiraling out of a nautilus in an unending, expanding growth pattern.

When we saw this, we immediately thought of soul mate love because this love, too, is an unending pattern of exponential growth.

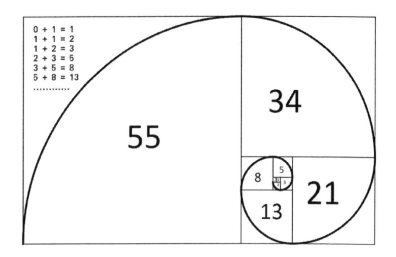

$$0 + 1 = 1$$
$$1 + 1 = 2$$
$$1 + 2 = 3$$
$$2 + 3 = 5$$
$$3 + 5 = 8$$
$$5 + 8 = 13$$

Follow the diagram from the small box to the spiraling, expanding area. This is how quantum soul mate love leaps occur.

What Scott saw in his regression is that we are all evolving in light more in line with this exponential Fibonacci sequence than in a simple incremental progression.

Here's a good example of exponential expansion in light.

Think of this. Not too long ago in the United States, the fastest way to travel was by horse and stagecoach.

Then came the train. The speed didn't just increase incrementally. It jumped exponentially.

And then came the plane – another exponential leap, to about 500 mph.

And then came our space travel to the moon and the space station orbiting the Earth and our space vehicles sent out to explore the universe – at over 25,000 miles per hour. This is exponential expansion.

This is the expansion you can envision and expect in your love life.

In soul living, there is no such thing as time. There is really only the present – no past and no future.

So get this. The expansion you might hope is possible for your life in the "future" is already present. Your next quantum leap is already here!

By making this assumption, you will see less incremental steps in your life and more synchronicities of soul mate love possibilities opening to you in the present.

The path of light

Even if your love life seems to be in the pits, don't envision a slow climbing out of the pit to something slightly better. Envision the Fibonacci sequence at work in your love life.

And if you seem to be repeating a pattern of love that is painfully the same, or only incrementally improving, open your heart to soul expansion.

Soul mate love is on the path of light.

As you merge with the accelerated light path, you too will experience the quality of rapid growth. As you've seen by now, soulmate love is exponentially powerful.

The sooner you see this, the sooner expansion of love can occur in your life – because your consciousness won't be mired in limitation or small thinking.

Our dream for you

This is our dream for you. Our evolution into the bliss of soul mate love gave us the opportunity to share this book with you. Now it's your turn for an exponential leap in love.

Everything in this book is possible for you. The light will open to you in different ways, because each of us is unique. But you are on a path of light that embraces soul mate love.

It is our hope that through our transparency, you will be able to discover your own soul, explore it, and begin to remember who you are as you live your life under this context of your soul. This is life changing!

Thank you for joining us in this journey of exploring soul mate love. And thank you for your beautiful, exquisite soul.

The universe needs the brightness and clarity and radiance of your soul. Your soul pods need you. And yes, your soul mate needs you.

Let this diagram of exponential expansion represent your leap into soul mate love.

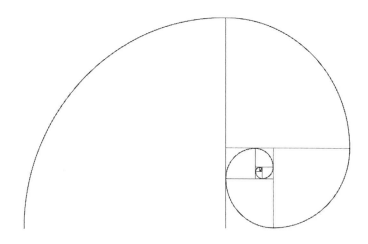

About the Authors

Shannon Peck was a spiritual healer for over 35 years. She is constantly expanding her soul awareness through avid reading of many appreciated authors who are dedicated to healing & soul growth. She also wrote a book, "Love Heals: How to Heal Everything with Love" to share what she had learned as a healer.

Shannon enjoys giving Between Lives Soul Regressions to those we live in or visit San Diego. You can learn more at www.ShannonPeck.com

Scott Peck has been a reporter, photographer, advertising manager, copywriter, educator, real estate broker, & author and has looked at each of these adventures as part of his "love career."

Together, they have shared their love insights through books, talks, & interviews with the high hope of awakening more love in people's hearts and on our planet.

Proof

Made in the USA
Columbia, SC
25 February 2018